JAPANESE COOKING

Gramercy Publishing Company • New York

JAPANESE COOKING
Peter and Joan Martin

FOREWORD BY SIR JOHN PILCHER K.C.M.G.

ILLUSTRATIONS BY CLIFTON KARHU

To MARIKO FUJIKAWA

who bore with us

this book is affectionately dedicated

This edition is published by Gramercy Publishing Company
a division of Crown Publishers, Inc.
by arrangement with Bobbs-Merrill
a b c d e f g h
Manufactured in the United States of America

CONTENTS

FOREWORD

by SIR JOHN PILCHER K.C.M.G.
H.M. Ambassador to Tokyo

To write about Japanese cooking is to discourse about Japanese aesthetics, philosophy and way of living. This is true in varying degrees of the food of every race and culture. It is particularly true of Japan. That quintessence of Japanese functions, the tea ceremony, is unthinkable without its surroundings: the room, which must be to a man what a nest is to a bird, neither too much nor too little; the natural-coloured wood, the plain, harmonious surfaces should produce the perfect setting for quiet recollection. The preparative wait on the bench in the subdued, evergreen garden, the climb through the low door prepare for the austere elegance and tranquil refinement within. The powdered green leaves exude the very essence of the tea plant's natural flavour. The movements in the preparation should be as natural and proper to a man as the unstudied, unpremeditated elegance of a cat moving instinctively without thought.

All Japanese cooking needs its setting. A Japanese meal is unthinkable without a quiet, withdrawn room looking on to the garden, which must be a picture to be seen from inside, beautiful at all seasons. The appropriate painting in the one alcove, the flower arrangement that should seem born rather than made, the table, the utensils, the movements of the waitresses as they open the sliding doors, all are essential ingredients in the pleasure which a Japanese meal provides. The quality of the tableware, the appropriateness of each vessel to its contents are studied to the last degree.

Freshness and a certain astringency are the qualities most prized. Like the English housewife, the Japanese will declare that their ingredients are so good that they need no sauce. Sauces, she would add, are anyway the product of decadence and bad materials; they are needed to shroud them and atone for their lack of natural fragrance.

The feast is for the eye and the mind. If you are still hungry, you slip round the corner and get a huge bowl of noodles steaming in an onion soup. It is vulgar to show hunger, which can be so easily assuaged. A Japanese banquet, like a tea ceremony, is food for the spirit. Mere eating can be done elsewhere. Mr and Mrs Martin, however, initiate you into the mysteries of both.

INTRODUCTION

Cookery books fall into two categories – those designed mainly for reading, and those intended to be used. This is, we hope, one of the latter. We have attempted in what follows to indicate the full range of Japanese cooking as well as to give authentic Japanese recipes, not, as so often happens, adaptations to what are fondly imagined to be western tastes. The only concession we have made to the western palate is to reduce considerably the amount of sugar called for in the original version of most recipes. The Japanese have tended in the past to like meat and vegetables far sweeter than we do, probably because, having no dessert dishes, they took in little sugar otherwise. However, in recent years, there has developed a tendency among the Japanese themselves to dislike excessive sugar in meats and vegetables and many a Japanese housewife will halve or even quarter the amount of sugar a recipe calls for, just as we have done in this book.

It is one of the unfortunate drawbacks in cooking any exotic foods that many ingredients are difficult if not impossible to obtain for those living outside large metropolitan areas. This is undoubtedly true of Japanese foodstuffs. Unlike both the Chinese and the Indians, the Japanese have only recently constituted a fairly sizeable expatriate group in England and the existence of such a community is probably necessary to make known, to popularize and to maintain standards of an alien cuisine. As a result there is probably no cuisine of any other major nation of which we remain so ignorant. Nevertheless, rather than tampering with the essence of many dishes by over-anglicizing them, we have written the recipes as they are prepared in Japan, trying to indicate in the section on ingredients substitutions which can be made. In any case misgivings are probably unduly stressed: you will find in practice that a great number of the dishes can be prepared from ingredients found on the shelves of any reasonably well-stocked grocer.

We have not included sections on desserts or *hors-d'oeuvres*. Although there are a variety of Japanese cakes there are no Japanese desserts. The cakes are usually eaten with tea at tea ceremonies, as snacks between meals, or occasionally as a prelude to a meal. They are complicated, and even the Japanese housewife herself seldom ventures into their preparation, it being considered a mark of greater expertise in the housewifely arts to know where to buy good cakes than how to make them. A Japanese meal, if terminated by anything other than plain boiled rice and pickles, is brought to a conclusion with a piece of fresh fruit, usually sculpted into fantastic forms.

A section on *hors-d'oeuvres* was omitted for the opposite reason. So many Japanese dishes are, in fact, *hors-d'oeuvres* that they could not conveniently be separated from the *entrées*. It will be easy to pick out those recipes in the sections on fish, meat and vegetables which can serve equally well as suitable accompaniments to drinks or as possible first courses.

A word about quantities. An effort has been made to make most recipes suitable for six persons, although it is difficult to know exactly what that means. A banquet often consists of ten or even fifteen courses, most of which consist of minute amounts exquisitely arranged on carefully chosen individual plates. On the other hand, for ordinary family dinners heartier portions are consumed, and it is with this type of cooking and eating in mind that these recipes were prepared. In these recipes one cup equals eight fluid ounces and spoon measurements should be regarded as level. All Japanese cooks, however, work a great deal by taste and, especially since the strength and flavour of such basic seasonings as soy sauce and *mirin* wine vary enormously from product to product, it is always wiser to rely on one's own sense of taste than on exact measurements.

Many good and patient friends have instructed and advised us during the preparation of this book, and we should like to express our particular thanks to Mrs Takako Namikawa, Mrs Kitako Saihara, Mrs Maki Yoshida and Mrs Miyako Inoue. The help given by Mrs Miyoko Fujinami and Mrs Michie Tanaka who gave us several of their own recipes is much appreciated. For many of the recipes given in this book we have been greatly indebted to Mrs Sumiko Sen's masterly *Nihon Ryori*, published by the Shufunotomo Magazine Company.

Our friend Mr Robert Strickland of the Ashiya Restaurant in Kyoto very kindly supplied the recipe for the 'drunk chicken' which is a specialty of his house, and we have received much valuable information about the problems of cooking in Japanese style in England from Miss Chise Kuzusaka of the Hiroko Restaurant in London and from Mr and Mrs Shiro Nakajo, who gave freely of their knowledge of housekeeping Japanese-style in London. To all these and to many others whose help and advice we may have neglected to acknowledge in adequate detail, we offer our sincere thanks.

PETER AND JOAN MARTIN

THE JAPANESE CUISINE

Writing at the time of the first Queen Elizabeth, the author of a description of 'The Kingdome of Japonica' remarks of the Japanese people that '. . . they delighte not much in fleshe, but they lyve for the most parte with herbes, fyshe, barley and ryce: which thinges are their chieffe nowrishments'. What was true of the sixteenth century is still largely true, though the relative abstinence from meat on the part of the twentieth century Japanese is now due more to its astronomically high price than to any lack of delight in it.

The Japanese cuisine has been much maligned, though probably unintentionally. The reasons are not hard to seek, and consist principally in the virtual insurmountability of the language barrier so far as the overwhelming majority of visitors are concerned, and the preference on the part of the Japanese for entertaining out, at restaurants, rather than in their own homes. Japanese generosity in hospitality is proverbial, and has the paradoxical disadvantage that foreigners are almost always taken by their Japanese hosts to expensive restaurants which restrict their offerings to a limited range of dishes thought to be elegant. This is apt to induce in the guest a feeling of simultaneous surfeit and disappointment, much as though one were to dine off canapés for a week.

The lucky few who speak Japanese or live in Japan long enough to explore the small eating houses favoured by the man in the street know better than to suppose that the tid-bits served in ceremonial style to honoured guests, even supplemented by the heartier meals of *sukiyak* and *tempura* which are thought to be more amenable to the foreign palate, are typical of what most people eat. It is our purpose in this book, therefore, not to ignore these dishes, but to point out the variety and extent of the Japanese cuisine, including the simple and honest dishes of the everyday diet which have been so neglected by westerners.

It is fashionable to attribute any departure from classical Japanese style in any sphere of life, whether it be clothes, amusements, architecture or food, to the baneful influence of the Americans since the war. Such a view is quite unhistorical. Throughout the centuries Japan has been the eager recipient of influences from overseas, and her two hundred years of virtual seclusion made the reaction after 1858 the more enthusiastic. Foreign customs were not always taken over very accurately (and in spite of General MacArthur and his cohorts it is *still* impossible to find a really good hamburger in Japan), but they were adopted very enthusiastically, and this is no new development.

One of the most popular kinds of cake in Japan is called *castera* and was introduced by the Portuguese in the sixteenth century; it is still a noted product of Nagasaki where it first found favour. The word is a corruption of *pan de Castilla*. The name of another very well-known dish, *tempura*, comes from the Portuguese *maigre*, or fare for Fridays. The ubiquitous 'curry-rice', which sometimes seems to be eaten for lunch by over ninety of Japan's hundred millions, was a feature of Tokyo life at least as long ago as the eighties of the last century, while *sukiyaki* itself was devised in the nineteenth century as a means of inducing ordinary Japanese to eat meat. Many other examples of culinary importations of great antiquity could be quoted, but enough has been said to demonstrate that 'pure Japanese style' in food is a chimaera, and always has been.

In practice, however, it is possible to draw a broad distinction between Japanese-style and western-style food in Japan, and to point out some of the main characteristics of the former. The latter is, perhaps mercifully, outside the scope of this book.

It has been pointed out many times that the primary appeal of Japanese food is to the eye, and though this is unquestionably true, it does not follow that this is its only appeal. Though flavours are generally delicate they are often subtly complex, and some distinctive specialities are superb.

There are interesting regional and ethnic variations also. To cite just a few examples, the Kyoto area is known for its vegetarian specialities and emphasis on the many different kinds of bean curd, while the sizeable Korean communities (including a numerous group in Kyoto) make splendid use of kidneys, liver, sweetbreads and other parts of animals which are regarded with a jaundiced eye by most Japanese. In the Nagasaki area of Kyushu, with its long trading history, Chinese influences are strong, while Osaka and Tokyo itself take pride in their splendid seafood and the fact that innovations generally spring up in one or the other of these cities.

The Japanese love esoteric mysteries of all kinds, and food and its preparation is surrounded by ritualistic folklore. Partly for this reason, most restaurants in Japan specialize in a very small range of dishes, sometimes only one. Thus there are places that sell nothing but noodles in various forms, others that offer only *tempura*, or crab, or *sushi*. We have more than once been assured in all seriousness that it takes ten years to learn to make *sushi*: during his lengthy probation the apprentice is limited to cooking the rice. It would be impertinent to deny the skill and dexterity of veteran Japanese cooks in their particular specialities, but we would nevertheless reassure the apprehensive that Japanese cooking is essentially no more difficult than any other, and a good deal easier than some.

Just as visual appeal is highly prized, so is freshness, and no self-respecting Japanese housewife omits a daily expedition to the market. In the case of fish, this is a hygienic necessity: in the case of less perishable foodstuffs it brings its own reward in superb fruit and vegetables and the only real chance to gossip with the neighbours.

As with Chinese food, the cooking process is usually brief, while preparation takes most of the time. Further, whatever has been cooked should generally be eaten as soon as possible, certainly within minutes and preferably within seconds. That this is very far from making it impossible to entertain guests to a home-cooked Japanese dinner is clearly demonstrated in the section on 'Cooking at the Table'.

Every day in Japan probably more than a hundred million pairs of *waribashi*, or light wooden chopsticks, are slid out of their paper envelopes, separated, used and thrown away. The lightweight Japanese chopsticks (including the washable lacquer kind) are easier to handle than the longer and heavier Chinese variety, and it is well worth the small effort to learn to use them. It is hard to say why the food tastes better from chopsticks than from western implements: one can only suggest the analogy of comparing wine out of a glass with wine from a tea cup. There is a fitness in things, and to enjoy Japanese food fully it is necessary to treat it politely.

DINING IN JAPANESE STYLE

European food –
Every blasted plate
is round.   (Anon: a modern *senryu*)

Traditional Japanese architecture and furnishings are so different from those of the West that it is virtually impossible outside Japan to reproduce the style of a formal dinner party. Bearing in mind, however, that even old-fashioned Japanese houses usually have one Western-style room, and that moderns tend more and more to westernize the old ways, the western hostess who serves Japanese food at an ordinary dining-room table is not so far out of step as she might imagine. The point has been reached where a good many ordinary folk in Japan would find a formal Japanese dinner party in the traditional style as unfamiliar as the western visitor coming to it for the first time, so remote is it from daily experience. Nevertheless, we venture a simple account of the basic essentials which the western hostess can adapt as conditions permit.

In a Japanese room there are, of course, no chairs, and the guests kneel, or in the case of men sit cross-legged, in their stockinged feet on large flat cushions (*zabuton*) placed directly on the *tatami* mats which form the floor. The Japanese table is about the height of a coffee table, and is usually used for dinner, though on very formal occasions each guest will have his own small lacquer tray with legs placed before him. The place of honour in a Japanese room is before the *tokonoma*, or alcove, which usually has a hanging scroll picture, flower arrangement or some other *objet d'art* placed in it. The hostess usually takes the place in front of the door, or on the opposite side of the table. Chopsticks are the only implements in sight, with the exception of the flat wooden paddle used for serving rice. Other spoons or forks are never used, except a flat china spoon sometimes used for *chawan mushi*.

A charming and refreshing preliminary to the meal is the presentation to each guest of tightly rolled hand towels dampened with very hot, sometimes scented water. It is perfectly in order to bury one's face in the towel for a few seconds as well as using it to wipe one's hands. The civilized pleasure to be derived from the *oshibori*, as it is called, makes converts of all who experience it.

Food is always served in individual lacquer or china bowls carefully chosen for shape and colour to suit the food which goes into them. Bowls should be lifted in the hand when eating from them. Since there are no spoons, soup is drunk straight from the bowl, chopsticks being used to eat the pieces of fish or vegetables often contained in it.

Our sixteenth-century commentator remarked of the Japanese: 'They have strong wine and rack distill'd of ryce, of which they will sometimes drinke largely, especially at their feasts and meetings. . . .' This is of course *sake*, which is now obtainable in the West. Etiquette prescribes that a guest should never charge his own glass, though it is proper and indeed desirable that he should perform that office for a neighbour. If *sake* is unobtainable, it would not be in any way outlandish to serve a medium dry white wine or a sweetish red wine in conventional western fashion with a Japanese meal. Our informant continues: 'As concern-ynge another drinke, they take great delighte in water mingled with a certaine powder which is very pretiouse, which they call CHIA.' This Japanese green tea is indeed an indispensable accompaniment to an in-formal meal. It is served from a kettle which is kept on the table and frequently replenished. China tea is a quite acceptable substitute.

The simplest basic Japanese dinner consists of a clear soup with tid-bits floating in it or a thick soup containing *miso*, followed by a main course, and ending with plain boiled rice and pickles. As we have already said, it is rare to have a dessert. If one is served at all it is almost always fresh fruit in season (or out of season if the host wishes to impress).

The *kaiseki* or 'company seat' is the grandest meal that most Japanese experience, and can range from seven courses to as many as twelve. Other quite formal meals include the *makunouchi bento*, which is essenti-ally a rather grand box lunch derived from the picnic-type lunches prepared for patrons to eat between the acts at theatrical performances, and various dishes appropriate to weddings, New Year festivities and other celebrations. Possibly nowhere else in the world is the progression of the seasons of the year more prized than in Japan, and the observant guest at a Japanese dinner will rarely fail to find delicate little touches in the decorations, such as an autumn leaf motif, symbolic snowflakes, summer flowers or the blossoms of spring at the appropriate times. With a little imagination the western hostess can add with equal grace to the pleasurable mood of guests enjoying good food and talk.

Boiled rice

Clear soup

Boiled foods

Sashimi (raw fish)
Sashimi dipping sauce

Sake cup

Tempura

Sake flask

Chopsticks
Chopstick rest

INGREDIENTS

The ingredients we have listed below are either those seasonings and basic materials essential to Japanese cooking, or those which are not well known in the West. Where possible, we have tried to indicate substitutes for those foods and seasonings not readily available in the West, but it should not be forgotten that the essential quality of the dish will be destroyed by too much tampering with its ingredients. Most of the ingredients referred to below, and all the essentials for Japanese cookery, may be obtained from the following suppliers:

NEW YORK:
Japanese Foodland, 2620 Broadway
Japanese Mart, 239 West 105th Street
Katagiri & Co., Inc., 224 East 59th Street
Oriental Food Shop, 1302 Amsterdam Avenue
Tanaka K. Co, Inc., 326 Amsterdam Avenue

CHICAGO:
Diamond Trading Co, 1108 Clark Street
Franklin Food Store, 1309 East 53rd Street
Star Market, 3349 North Clark Street
Toguri Mercantile Co., 5324 North Clark Street
York Super Food Market, 3240 North Clark Street

LOS ANGELES:
Enbun Co., 2313 West Jefferson Blvd.
Enbun Co., 248 East First Street
Ginza Market, 2600 West Jefferson Blvd.
Granada Market, 1820 Sawtelle Blvd. (West L.A.)
Meiji, 1569 West Redondo Beach Blvd, Gardena
Rafu Bussan Co., 344 East First Street
Safe and Save Japanese Market, 2030 Sawtelle Blvd. (West L.A.)

SAN FRANCISCO AREA:
Aloha Super Market, 14146 Almaden Road, San Jose
K. Sakai Co., 1656 Post Street, San Francisco
Nak's Oriental Market, 1151 Chestnut Street Menlo Park

AJI-NO-MOTO. A seasoning based on monosodium glutamate and designed to bring out the flavour of foods without adding any distinctive flavour of its own. It is a favourite stand-by of Japanese cooks and is used by them in almost all dishes. The western product *Accent*, the Chinese *Ve-Tsin*, or any monosodium glutamate powder can be used instead.

BEAN CURD (*tōfu*). A mild-flavoured, almost custard-like product made from the cooking, mashing and filtering of white soy beans, pressed into cakes. Bean curd is practically pure protein, and until quite recently was the principal source of protein in the Japanese diet. Three main types of *tōfu* are in common use: the plain, white variety called, simply, *tōfu*; *yakidōfu* which is grilled slightly on both sides; and *aburage*, bean curd which has been fried in deep fat. *Tōfu* is available fresh, and all three types of bean curd are available tinned.

BONITO, DRIED (*katsuobushi*). This is the basic ingredient of the basic Japanese soup stock called *dashi* (*see* page 30). The bonito fish is dried slowly until it resembles a stick of wood in both appearance and hardness. It is shaved to make the soup, and these packaged shavings, called *hanagatsuo*, can be purchased as a time saver.

BURDOCK ROOT (*gobō*). A long, slender root vegetable which is pared and used as an ingredient in many boiled or braised dishes.

DEVIL'S TONGUE (*konnyaku*). The roots of this vegetable are first turned into a starch, then into a translucent cake called *konnyaku*, or into spaghetti-like lengths called *shirataki* or *ito-konnyaku*, which is one of the main ingredients of *sukiyaki*. In Japan it is sold wet in plastic containers, and it is available in tins in the West.

CHRYSANTHEMUM LEAVES (*shungiku*). The tender leaves of the plant *chrysanthemum coronarium* are frequently used in casserole dishes and in soups. Fresh spinach leaves may be substituted, but since the stronger flavour of spinach can affect the other ingredients in a casserole it should be used with discretion.

FISH SAUSAGE (*kamaboko*). A mixture of pounded whitefish, corn-flour and rice wine which is sliced and used in soups and casseroles. It is often dyed a rather violent pink or green. A tinned variety is obtainable in the West.

GINGER (*shōga*). Fresh ginger roots are grated or sliced and used in soup and sauces. The long, slender ginger shoots are also eaten, and with their delicate hues of pink and white make a beautiful and delicious garnish.

GINGKO NUT (*ginnan*). These are the seeds of the tree *gingko biloba* which are peeled and simmered before being used. They are available tinned and ready to use.

HORSERADISH, JAPANESE (*wasabi*). Japanese horseradish is similar to the European variety, but slightly stronger and, in its powdered form, green in colour. Freshly grated, it is used as a garnish for raw fish and *sushi*, and as an ingredient in dipping sauces. It is also available powdered in tins. This powdered *wasabi* is mixed with water to a mustard-like consistency and allowed to stand for a few minutes before use.

LOTUS ROOT (*renkon*). The lotus root is pared, sliced, and used in various casseroles, or parboiled, dressed with vinegar and served as a salad. Tinned lotus root is on sale in the West.

MUSHROOMS. Two main types of mushrooms are used in Japan. The most highly prized are *matsutake*, or pine mushrooms, so named because they grow exclusively in pine forests. Even in season they are extremely expensive and are considered by the Japanese to be one of their greatest delicacies. The second, *shiitake*, is a large, flat, dark mushroom of strong flavour. Dried mushrooms, available in most large supermarkets, are a suitable substitute for *shiitake*, and although the Japanese would deny that anything can be substituted for *matsutake*, fresh champignon make quite an acceptable alternative in most dishes. The best substitute is the German *Steinpilz* or the French *cèpe* (more exactly, *cèpe de Bordeaux*).

NOODLES (*menrui*). Noodles served in broth with various toppings are among the most popular of luncheon snacks in Japan. *Soba*, a brown noodle made from buckwheat flour, and *udon*, thick, white noodles made from wheat flour, are the two most common varieties. Other types include *sōmen*, a very fine noodle made from wheat flour, and *harusame*, a fine, translucent noodle made from potatoes which is used mainly in cold dishes. In Japan both *udon* and *soba* are sold fresh and still damp, but all of these varieties of noodles are also available dried and are sold in the West. Lasagne noodles can be substituted for *udon* with great success.

SANSHO SPICE. This spice is made from the dried and powdered leaves of the prickly ash. It is only mildly hot, and is a favourite seasoning for noodle dishes and soups. It is available in bottles.

SEVEN-FLAVOURS SPICE (*shichimi-tōgarashi*). A blend of pepper leaf, poppy seed, rape seed, hemp seed, dried tangerine peel, and sesame seed which is used as a garnish and to sprinkle as a seasoning on noodle and rice dishes. According to the blend it ranges from a rather mild to a very hot, tangy flavour. It is available in both bottles and tins in the West.

OILS. For all types of cooking the Japanese prefer vegetable oils to animal fats. Both soy bean oil and corn oil are in common use. Both of these oils have little flavour of their own, and when a stronger flavour is desired part sesame seed oil is used.

RADISH, JAPANESE (*daikon*). The enormous, white radishes of Japan grow to an average size of a foot in length and seven or eight inches in width. In flavour they are similar to but slightly milder than the icicle radish of the West. *Daikon* is grated and used as a garnish or as one of the ingredients in dipping sauces, and is also a favourite vegetable for pickling. Fresh *daikon* is on sale at specialized shops in the West.

RICE WINE (*sake*). Besides being the usual accompaniment to Japanese meals, small quantities of *sake* are also used as a seasoning in many dishes. Beware of buying *sake* abroad for it does not keep more than a year, though an opened bottle will not spoil for several weeks.

RICE WINE (*mirin*). *Mirin* is a sweetened *sake* which is never drunk, but is used exclusively in cooking. It gives Japanese food one of its most characteristic flavours, but if something must be substituted for it try a dry sherry of reasonable quality, increasing slightly the amount of sugar called for in the recipe.

SEAWEEDS. The Japanese use a variety of processed and dried seaweed in many dishes, and the large quantity of iodine which they therefore consume is said to be the reason why goitre is almost non-existent in the Japanese archipelago. The most common types are the following.

PURPLE LAVER (*nori*), a black seaweed dried in paper-thin sheets and used as a wrapping for *sushi* and as a garnish for salads and raw fish.

KELP (*kombu*), which is one of the two basic ingredients in Japanese soup stock (*see* page 30). It is also used in making a simple stock for certain dishes such as simmered bean curd.

LOBE-LEAF (*wakame*), a dark green seaweed which is bought fresh or dried (when it is softened in water). It is used in both soups and salads.

SESAME SEEDS (*goma*). Both black and white sesame seeds are used in a variety of dishes. They are parched in a dry heavy frying pan until they begin to jump, then used either whole or crushed in order to release their flavour.

SOY SAUCE (*shōyū*). This is the most basic of Japanese seasonings. There are two types in common use. *Usukuchi*, or light soy sauce, is the lighter in colour and the more delicately flavoured. It is used in soups, custards, and other dishes where it is important not to muddy the colour. *Koikuchi*, or dark soy sauce, is a thick, strong sauce used for grilling foods and as an ingredient in certain sauces. Most soy sauces produced in the West are much stronger and thicker than both types of Japanese soy sauce, and it is strongly recommended that Japanese soy sauce be used. If this is not possible, however, use western varieties with a sparing hand, for amounts given in this book are for the Japanese product. Also bear in mind that soy sauce contains salt, and that in any dish containing soy sauce very little salt is needed.

SOYBEAN PASTE (*miso*). *Miso* is used in almost all types of Japanese dishes: as a soup, it is the traditional breakfast, and sweetened it forms the most basic Japanese cake. It can be bought in tins and if stored in the refrigerator it will keep for a year or more. The various types are *shiro-miso*, sweet, white, and lightly salted; *inaka-miso*, beige in colour and slightly saltier; *aka-miso*, red and lightly salted; *sendai-miso*, red and heavily salted; and *hatcho-miso*, the only bean paste made entirely of soybeans and very rich in protein.

VINEGAR (*su*). Japanese vinegar is distilled from rice and has a certain lightness and sweetness in its flavour that is totally lacking in western vinegars. A distilled cider vinegar may be used as a substitute, with a slight increase in the amount of sugar called for. You may also need less vinegar than the recipe calls for.

UTENSILS

DONABE. An earthenware casserole with a lid, which is glazed inside and unglazed out. It can be placed over direct heat and is used in many of the dishes such as *shabu-shabu* and *mizudaki* described in the section on 'Cooking at the Table'. These dishes should be heated and cooled slowly as any sudden changes in temperature are likely to cause cracking.

SUKIYAKI-NABE. A round, flat-bottomed, cast-iron pan used for cooking *sukiyaki*. It should be coated with a thin film of oil before storing. Any heavy, preferably cast-iron frying pan is a suitable substitute.

TEPPAN. A flat, rectangular iron plate which is used in cooking steak, fish, and vegetables *teppan-yaki* style. Like a griddle, it should not be washed, but wiped off with an oiled cloth until clean. A large griddle is a very effective substitute.

CHŪKA-NABE. Originally Chinese, this useful pan is used for both sautéeing and for deep-fat frying. It is large enough for food to be tossed about in it without coming out. It is also economical of cooking oil in deep-fat frying since the area of the cooking surface is much greater than that of the bottom of the pan.

ZARU. A bamboo basket used for draining and/or straining. Any western colander or strainer is a suitable substitute.

SUDARE. A mat of fine bamboo slats used for rolling *sushi*, omelets, and vegetables. The bamboo is strong, yet flexible, and the spaces between the slats allow moisture to escape. An old bamboo tablemat of the slat variety can be substituted.

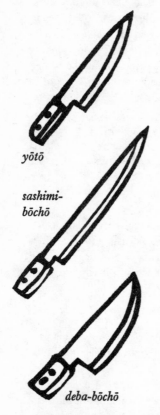

yōtō

sashimi-bōchō

deba-bōchō

KNIVES. Japanese knives are superb and the Japanese use of the knife has reached the level of a minor art. In a single, lightning-quick blur the expert cook can produce a series of uniformly thin slices which could rival in speed and appearance those produced by the fanciest slicing machine. The knives are heavy and sharp, and the secret is to keep the point of the knife stationary, raising the back and letting the weight of the knife itself do most of the cutting. The food should be moved through the knife, not the knife over the food. Japanese knives are designed for at variety of purposes. The *yōtō* is used for general purpose cutting and slicing; the *sashimi-bōchō* for slicing raw fish, or for slicing any very soft material into very fine slices; and the *deba-bōchō* for heavy chopping, cutting the heads off fish, and so forth.

SURIBACHI and **SURIKOGI.** These are the Japanese version of the mortar and pestle. An earthenware bowl, serrated inside, which very effectively aids any process of grinding or pulverizing.

CHOPSTICKS. Assorted lengths of chopsticks, both bamboo and metal, are used in cooking. They are excellent for frying and for mixing ingredients into rice when a spoon or heavier implement is apt to mash the food. It is well worth the effort involved in learning how to use them.

SHAMOJI. A wide, flat serving spoon for rice made of varnished wood or bamboo. Rice does not adhere to it as much as to an ordinary spoon, nor does it mash the rice.

TAMAGO-YAKI NABE. Rectangular frying pan used for frying omelets. Omelets are often rolled and this shape naturally produces an omelet which can be more neatly rolled than those cooked in round pans.

PICKLE BARREL AND LID. Used for preparing salted pickles. The lid is always slightly smaller in diameter than the barrel itself, so that it can be placed directly on top of the ingredients to be pickled.

OSHIWAKU. Wooden press used in making *oshizushi*.

SOUPS

'Soup of the evening, beautiful Soup!'
LEWIS CARROLL

Like all other civilized peoples, the Japanese are extremely fond of soup, and have evolved, as in the West, the two main types of clear and thick. The clear soups are far less complicated and time-consuming to make than the consommés of the West, and at first sight may seem proportionately less interesting. Any such impression is a mistake, for the rich intensity of flavour of Japanese clear soups, their clarity and the beauty of their garnishes make them a fitting rival of anything found in the West, and quite worthy and appropriate as the first course even of a formal western meal.

The thick soups of Japan fall into two sub-classes, those containing hearty additions of meat and vegetables, and those thickened with *miso* or bean paste. Though *miso* soups have a very distinctive flavour, not always immediately appealing to westerners, they are undoubtedly the most popular of soups in Japan, and form the indispensable basis of the traditional Japanese breakfast.

DASHI (*Japanese Soup Stock*)

The so-called *dashi* broth is the basis of almost all Japanese soups, as well as of most casseroles, stews, sauces, and so forth. Although its preparation is unfamiliar to western housewives, it is easy and quick once the ingredients are purchased. They can be had at any shop dealing in Japanese foodstuffs. You will probably be shown two types of bonito fillet (*katsuobushi*): one resembling a block of dried wood, the other ready shaved and packaged, called *hanagatsuo*. By all means use the packaged variety as shaving a dried bonito fillet is a lengthy job requiring a special tool.

6 cups water   ½ oz kelp, *kombu* seaweed
½ oz shaved dried bonito fillet,
   katsuobushi

Bring the water to the boil and add the seaweed. Stir it around in the water for three or four minutes in order to release its flavour. Remove the seaweed and add the bonito shavings. Bring to the boil again, then immediately remove from the fire. Allow the shavings to settle to the bottom of the pan; this will take only two or three minutes. Strain, and the broth is ready to use.

There are also available on the market packets of instant *dashi* broth, usually mixed in the proportion of one cup water to one packet *dashi* powder. Some brands are quite good, and they do reduce the process of making the broth to one of the utmost simplicity.

CHICKEN STOCK

Although the distinctive flavour of *dashi* is characteristic of so many Japanese dishes, when its ingredients cannot be found this chicken stock may be substituted. It is also the stock used for certain dishes such as *mizutaki*.

1 lb chicken   2 teaspoons salt
1 lb chicken bones   1 teaspoon monosodium
2 spring onions   glutamate
1 2-inch piece fresh ginger root   2 quarts water

Slice the ginger into thin pieces and cut the spring onions, including their green tops, into inch-long pieces. Chop the chicken into pieces. Put all the ingredients into a soup kettle and bring to the boil. Reduce heat and simmer for about one hour. Several times during the simmering skim the surface of its residue. Cool, taste for seasoning and correct as necessary. Remove any fat, and strain through a cloth in order to obtain a clear broth. The soup stock is now ready to use.

HAMAGURI USHIOJIRU (Clam Consommé)

About 30 live clams	1½ tablespoons *sake*
6 cups water	1 teaspoon monosodium
2 teaspoons salt	glutamate

Wash the clams thoroughly in running water, brushing the edges to make sure that no sand or grit adheres to them. Put the clams and the water into a saucepan and heat until the clams open. Discard any which don't open. Add the seasonings, and the soup is ready to serve. Do not simmer the soup for long after the clams have opened or they will become hard and tasteless.

SAKANA USHIOJIRU (Fish Consommé)

1 lb trimmings, bones, head and tail of any white fish	1 teaspoon salt
6–8 cups water	½ teaspoon monosodium glutamate
2 tablespoons *sake*	¾ cup finely chopped spring onions, including tops
1–2 tablespoons light soy sauce	

Put the water and fish into a saucepan and bring to a full, rolling boil. Lower the heat and skim the surface until clear. This soup does not need to simmer for very long, and ten minutes should be enough. Strain into a clean saucepan and discard the fish. Taste and correct if necessary. Place in the bottom of each soup bowl two tablespoons or more finely chopped spring onions. Bring the soup to the boil again and ladle about one cup of the boiling broth into each bowl. Serve immediately.

CLEAR SOUP WITH HERRINGS

6 cups *dashi* or other fish stock
1 teaspoon salt
2 teaspoons light soy sauce
½ teaspoon monosodium glutamate
6 pieces fresh herring fillets

6 large fresh mushrooms
18–24 fresh chrysanthemum or
   spinach leaves
1 lemon

Cut the fish fillets into halves lengthwise so that you have twelve narrow strips. Salt lightly and tie each strip into a simple, overlapping knot. Secure with a toothpick and drop into boiling water for two to three minutes. Remove and keep warm. Wash the mushrooms and cut away the stems. Score the tops lightly several times and sprinkle with a little light soy sauce. Wash the chrysanthemum or spinach leaves and cut off their stems. Use only perfect leaves. Cut six thin lengths of peel from a lemon, each strip about ¼ inch wide and 1½ inches long.

Bring the *dashi* and salt to the boil and while boiling add the soy sauce and monosodium glutamate. Taste for seasoning and correct if necessary. Add the mushrooms and simmer for three minutes. While the mushrooms are cooking, dip the chrysanthemum leaves into the boiling soup for a few seconds, until just soft. Arrange two pieces of the fish, one mushroom, a few chrysanthemum leaves, and piece of the lemon peel in each bowl. Ladle the boiling stock over the top and serve immediately.

CLEAR SOUP WITH QUAIL EGG AND
VEGETABLES

6 cups *dashi* or chicken broth
1 teaspoon salt
6 quail eggs
1 stalk celery

1 small carrot
2 teaspoons light soy sauce
¼ teaspoon monosodium glutamate
2 tablespoons chopped chives

Hard-boil the quail eggs and remove their shells. Cut the carrot and celery into julienne strips and boil separately in salted water until just tender. Chop the chives finely. Heat the *dashi*. When it comes to the boil add salt, monosodium glutamate, and soy sauce. Taste for seasoning and correct if necessary. Arrange about one teaspoon each of the carrots, celery, and chives with one whole quail's egg in each bowl and pour the boiling broth on top. Serve immediately.

CLEAR SOUP WITH BAMBOO SHOOTS AND SEAWEED

6 cups *dashi* or chicken broth	2 teaspoons light soy sauce
1 small bamboo shoot	Salt
2 6-inch pieces *wakame* seaweed	Monosodium glutamate

The young, tender tips of bamboo shoots are best for this soup, but any kind will do. Slice the bamboo shoot into thin pieces, about $\frac{1}{2}$ inch wide and no more than $\frac{1}{8}$ inch thick. Sprinkle with a little soy sauce and let them stand while the stock is heating. Cover the *wakame* seaweed with cold water and let it stand until soft, about twenty minutes. Slice into pieces the same size as the bamboo shoots. Heat the *dashi* and when it comes to the boil add the soy sauce and salt and monosodium glutamate to taste. Taste for seasoning and correct if necessary. Add the bamboo shoots and simmer for five minutes. Place a little of the *wakame* seaweed in the bottom of each bowl and pour over the top the boiling stock and bamboo shoots. Serve immediately.

CLEAR SOUP WITH CHICKEN AND MUSHROOMS

6 cups chicken stock	1 lemon
$\frac{3}{4}$ lb boned chicken	Salt
6 large fresh mushrooms,	2 tablespoons cornflour
matsutake variety if available	2 tablespoons *sake*

Cut the boned chicken into twelve pieces of roughly equal size. Salt lightly, sprinkle with the *sake* and allow to stand for twenty minutes. Wash the mushrooms, trim off the tough part of the stems and slice each into four pieces. Drain the chicken, reserving the *sake* in which it has been marinating. Roll the chicken in the cornflour, drop into boiling water and poach until done. Do not overcook. Remove and reserve. Bring the chicken stock to the boil, add the *sake* marinade, and taste for seasoning, adding salt and a little soy sauce if necessary. Add the mushrooms to the stock and simmer for four or five minutes until they are tender. Remove and arrange four slices of mushroom and two pieces of chicken in each bowl. Ladle the boiling broth over the top and garnish with a thin strip of lemon zest.

2

CLEAR SOUP WITH CHICKEN AND
WATERCRESS

6 cups chicken broth   2 tablespoons *sake*
2 teaspoons light soy sauce   1 teaspoon salt
½ lb chicken, cut from the bone   Monosodium glutamate
1 bunch watercress or *mitsuba*
  (trefoil) leaves

Cut the chicken into thin slices and sprinkle lightly with salt and the
sake. Wash the watercress or *mitsuba* and chop coarsely. Bring the broth
and soy sauce to the boil and taste for seasoning, correcting if necessary.
Add the slices of chicken and the *sake* in which it has been marinating
to the boiling stock and simmer for five minutes or until the chicken is
done. Add the watercress or *mitsuba* and simmer for one minute longer.
Ladle into bowls and serve immediately.

HAMAGURI TO SHIITAKE USHIOJIRU
(Clam and Mushroom Soup)

20–30 live clams   1½ tablespoons *sake*
6 cups water   6 large fresh mushrooms
1 teaspoon salt   12 leaves fresh spinach
2 teaspoons light soy sauce   Lemon peel
Monosodium glutamate

Wash the clams thoroughly under running water, brushing to remove
all sand and grit. Put the clams and water into a saucepan and heat until
the clams open. Discard any which do not open. Remove the clams from
the broth and take them out of their shells. Choose the six most perfect
shells and put all the clams into these six shells. Reserve in a warm
place. Wash the mushrooms and trim off any hard pieces on the stems.
Cut into thin slices. Wash the spinach carefully, choosing attractive
leaves, and cutting off all but ½ inch of the stem. Cut six lengths of
lemon peel, about ⅛ inch wide and 2 inches long. Bring the clam stock
to the boil again and add the seasonings of salt, soy sauce, *sake*, and
monosodium glutamate. Taste for seasoning and correct if necessary.
Add the mushrooms and cook for three or four minutes. Add the spinach
leaves and lemon peel and cook thirty seconds longer. Put one clam shell

filled with clams in each soup bowl and pour the boiling broth over the top. Carefully arrange two of the spinach leaves across the centre of the clam shell and surround with the mushrooms and the length of lemon peel. Serve immediately.

CLEAR SOUP WITH BEAN CURD AND SPRING ONIONS

6 cups *dashi* or chicken stock
1 piece bean curd, *tōfu*
  (about 1 lb)
2 spring onions

1 lemon
2 teaspoons light soy sauce
Salt
Monosodium glutamate

Drain the bean curd and cut into twelve squares, roughly 1½ inches each. Slice the spring onions, including tops, into fine rings. Slice thin lengths of peel from the lemon. Bring the *dashi* to the boil and add the soy sauce and salt and monosodium glutamate to taste. Add the bean curd and simmer slowly until it is heated through. Remove carefully and put two squares in each soup bowl, sprinkling over the top a spoonful of the chopped spring onion and adding a length of the lemon peel. Carefully pour in the boiling broth and serve immediately.

KAKITAMA-JIRU (Egg Drop Soup)

6 cups *dashi* or chicken broth
1 teaspoon salt
3 tablespoons light soy sauce
3 eggs

2 dozen small snow peas or ½ cup
  green peas
Monosodium glutamate

Boil the snow peas or green peas in salted water until tender. Drain and reserve. Bring the stock to the boil and add salt, soy sauce, and monosodium glutamate. Taste for seasoning and correct if necessary. Beat the eggs well and pour them in a thin stream into the centre of the boiling stock. Keep the broth moving in a slow whirlpool with a spoon so that the eggs will remain suspended as they cook. They will cook in thread-like segments. Pour into soup bowls, garnish with the green peas or snow peas and serve immediately.

CLEAR SOUP WITH NOODLES AND CHICKEN

6 cups chicken stock	2 dried mushrooms
3 oz dried *sōmen* noodles or some other thin noodle	2 tablespoons *sake*
	2 teaspoons light soy sauce
½ lb boned chicken	Salt
1 spring onion	Monosodium glutamate

Wash and clean the spring onion and chop finely. Soak the mushrooms in cold water until soft, discard the stems and chop the caps. Cut the chicken into cubes, sprinkle with the *sake* and salt lightly. Cook the noodles according to the recipe on page 63 and reserve. Bring the chicken stock to the boil and add the soy sauce, salt, and monosodium glutamate to taste. Add the mushrooms and chicken, including the *sake* in which it has been marinating, and simmer for three or four minutes or until the chicken is done. Pour boiling water over the noodles to re-heat them, drain and arrange in the bottom of the soup bowls. Pour the boiling soup over them and garnish with the chopped spring onion. Serve immediately.

CLEAR SOUP WITH PRAWN AND WATERCRESS

6 cups *dashi* or chicken stock	1 bunch watercress
2 teaspoons soy sauce	Salt
12 prawns	Monosodium glutamate
2 tablespoons cornflour	

Shell and de-vein the prawns, leaving the tails intact. Wash carefully and salt lightly. Arrange the prawns in pairs, interlocking the thick ends so that a circle is formed with the tails on opposite sides. Skewer with a toothpick. Roll in the cornflour until well-covered. Drop into boiling water and cook until they turn pink, no more than two or three minutes. Remove, drain and carefully remove the toothpicks. Reserve in a warm place. Bring the *dashi* or chicken stock to the boil and add the soy sauce and salt and monosodium glutamate to taste. Coarsely chop the watercress. Place the pairs of prawns in the bottom of six soup bowls, add the chopped watercress and cover with the boiling broth. Serve immediately.

CLEAR SOUP WITH CUSTARD

6 cups *dashi* or chicken stock
2 teaspoons light soy sauce
4 oz fresh spinach
1 lemon
Salt

6 eggs
1 cup *dashi* or chicken stock
1½ teaspoons light soy sauce
½ teaspoon sugar
Monosodium glutamate

Make the custard by beating the eggs well and adding one cup of the soup stock, 1½ teaspoons light soy sauce, the sugar, and a dash of monosodium glutamate. Mix well, strain, and pour into a square mould. Cook the custard until firm, either by steaming over a low flame or in a low oven. Cool and carefully unmould. Cut the custard into six squares.

Bring the stock to the boil and taste for seasoning, adding the soy sauce and salt if necessary. Wash the spinach and cook separately in salted water until tender. Drain well, and cut into lengths slightly shorter than the width of the custard squares. Cut six neat lengths of lemon peel, each about ¼ inch wide and 1 inch long. In the soup bowls arrange a square of the custard with a length of the spinach on top of it, and in the centre of the spinach a piece of lemon peel. Carefully ladle the boiling broth over the top and serve immediately.

SPINACH AND PORK SOUP

8 cups water
1 lb piece of lean pork,
    preferably tenderloin
⅓ cup light soy sauce

6 oz fresh spinach
1 teaspoon salt
½ teaspoon white pepper
1 1-inch piece fresh ginger root

Marinate the pork in the soy sauce for one hour. Bring the water to the boil and add the pork and its soy sauce marinade, simmering until the pork is done. Remove the piece of pork, reserving the stock. Add the salt and pepper. Grate the ginger root, squeeze the pulp and add the juice produced to the stock. Taste for seasoning and correct if necessary. Shred the pork by hand, pulling it apart into thin strips about an inch long. Add the pork to the stock and heat. Wash the spinach and coarsely cut it into pieces roughly an inch square. Add the spinach to the stock and cook for a further minute. Serve immediately. This soup may also be garnished with a one-egg omelet, fried thin and cut into strips.

WATERCRESS AND PORK SOUP

Substitute for the spinach two bunches of watercress (or, in Japan, *seri*). Chop coarsely and proceed as above.

OZŌNI

Ozōni is the soup which is traditionally served on New Year's Day. Each district of Japan has its own variant of the dish, the only constant being that it must include a piece of *omochi*, that dense, glutinous rice cake which is inseparable from New Year celebrations.

6 cups *dashi* or chicken stock
6 *omochi* rice cakes
1 bamboo shoot
¾ lb boned chicken
4 oz chrysanthemum leaves or watercress

1 6-inch piece fish sausage, *kamaboko* (optional)
2 tablespoons *sake*
2 teaspoons light soy sauce
Salt
Monosodium glutamate

Slice the chicken into thin pieces and sprinkle lightly with salt and *sake*. Cut the bamboo shoot into slices about ⅛ inch thick. Bring the soup stock to the boil, add the soy sauce and salt and monosodium glutamate to taste. While the soup stock is heating grill the rice cakes until they are soft, taking care that they do not burn. Slice the fish sausage into ¼-inch thick pieces. Put these, the bamboo shoots and the chicken into the stock and simmer for five minutes. Add the washed chrysanthemum leaves or watercress, coarsely chopped, and cook for a few seconds longer. Place a hot rice cake in each soup bowl, ladle the hot soup over the top and serve immediately.

CLEAR SOUP WITH PORK AND VEGETABLES

6 cups chicken stock
½ lb lean pork
1 small carrot
4 dried mushrooms
1 small bamboo shoot
1 medium potato

2 tablespoons green peas
2 tablespoons light soy sauce
Salt
White pepper
Monosodium glutamate

Cut the pork in ¼-inch cubes, sprinkle with a little soy sauce and let stand for fifteen minutes. Soak the mushrooms in cold water until soft and trim away any tough stems. Reserve the water in which the mushrooms soaked. Peel the potato, scrape the carrot and wash the bamboo shoot, then cut all the vegetables, including the mushrooms, into ¼-inch cubes. Boil them separately in salted water until tender but not soft. Drain, and reserve in a warm place. Bring the *dashi* or chicken stock to the boil, add soy sauce to taste, the water from the mushrooms and a dash of monosodium glutamate. Add the drained pork cubes and simmer until done, three or four minutes. Add a dash of salt and pepper, taste for seasoning and correct if necessary. Distribute the vegetables among six soup bowls, pour the boiling broth and pork over the top and serve immediately.

WAKATAKEJIRU (Bamboo Shoot and Wakame Seaweed Soup)

This is particularly delicious in the spring when the bamboo shoots are young and tender.

6 cups *dashi* or chicken stock	6 leaves *kinome*, Japanese pepper
1 boiled bamboo shoot or 1 tin bamboo shoots	(optional)
¼ cup light soy sauce	Salt
1 oz *wakame* seaweed (if not available substitute spinach)	Monosodium glutamate

Fresh spring bamboo shoots are to be preferred for this soup, but tinned ones may, of course, be substituted. If fresh bamboo shoots are available, prepare by washing away any dirt which clings to them and boiling them in their skins in salted water until tender, about thirty minutes. Remove, drain and when cool enough to handle remove their skins. If tinned bamboo shoots are used simply drain carefully.

Soak the *wakame* seaweed in cold water for twenty minutes or until soft. Drain and cut into pieces about ½ inch wide and 1½ inches long. Cut the bamboo shoots into slices of a similar size. If you substitute spinach for the seaweed, wash it carefully and cook in boiling water until just tender. Drain well and cut into 1½-inch lengths. Bring the

soup stock to the boil and add salt, soy sauce and monosodium glutamate. Taste for seasoning and correct if necessary. Add the bamboo
shoots and seaweed to the boiling broth and simmer for ten minutes.
If spinach is being used, do not add it to the broth, but keep warm and
arrange in the bottom of the soup bowls, pouring the hot broth and
bamboo shoots over it. Decorate with the *kinome* leaves if available, and
serve immediately.

KUZUHIKI SOUP

6 cups *dashi* broth	Salt
1 piece bean curd, *tōfu* (about 1 lb)	Monosodium glutamate
1½ tablespoons cornflour	1-inch piece of fresh ginger root
1 tablespoon soy sauce	

Bring the broth to the boil and add the seasonings of soy sauce and
monosodium glutamate. Taste for seasoning and add a little salt if
necessary. Dissolve the cornflour in a little cold water, add to the soup
and cook until slightly thickened. Cut the bean curd into six pieces and
add carefully. Simmer for about five minutes or until the bean curd is
heated through. Put a piece of bean curd in each soup bowl and pour
the hot soup over the top. Put a small spoonful of grated ginger in the
centre of the bean curd and serve immediately.

NOPPEI-JIRU (Vegetable Soup)

This hearty vegetable soup is well-suited to cold winter days.

6 cups *dashi* or chicken stock	6 mushrooms
4 oz Japanese radish, *daikon*	2 tablespoons light soy sauce
4 oz carrots	1 teaspoon salt
1 small turnip	Monosodium glutamate
1 oz kidney beans	2 tablespoons cornflour
1 piece fried bean curd, *aburage*	

Soak the kidney beans in cold water for several hours, removing any
which float to the surface. Boil in salted water until just tender. Cut the

daikon radish, the carrot and the turnip into ½-inch cubes. Dip the fried bean curd into boiling water for a few seconds in order to remove its excess oil. Cut into ½-inch widths. Cut the mushrooms into pieces of the same size.

In a large saucepan bring the soup stock to the boil and add the carrots, *daikon* radish, turnip, and fried bean curd. Simmer for fifteen to twenty minutes, or until the vegetables are tender. Add the mushrooms and the kidney beans, and the seasonings of salt, soy sauce, and monosodium glutamate. Taste and correct seasoning if necessary. Dissolve the cornflour in a little water and add to the boiling soup, stirring until it thickens slightly. Serve very hot.

The fried bean curd is sometimes cooked before it is added to the soup to improve its flavour. Simmer for ten minutes in ⅓ cup broth, 2 tablespoons soy sauce, and 1 tablespoon sugar, then add to the soup.

KENCHIN-JIRU (Chicken and Vegetable Soup)

6 cups *dashi* or chicken stock	4 oz carrot
1 square of bean curd, *tōfu*	2 tablespoons oil
(about 1 lb)	1–2 teaspoons salt
6 oz boned chicken	2 tablespoons light soy sauce
2 oz burdock root	Monosodium glutamate
6 dried mushrooms	¼ teaspoon red pepper (optional)
2 oz *daikon* radish	

Wrap the bean curd in a clean kitchen cloth and press lightly to remove the excess water. Scrape the carrot and burdock root and peel the *daikon*. Cut them all into julienne strips, putting the burdock root into cold water to prevent discoloration. Soak the mushrooms in cold water until soft; remove their tough stems and cut into strips.

Heat the oil in the bottom of a heavy-bottomed saucepan. Break the bean curd into pieces and drop it into the hot oil. Let it sizzle for a minute or so, turning over lightly with a wooden spoon or spatula. Add the chicken and let it fry for a few minutes longer. Pour in the hot stock, add the vegetables and then season with the salt, soy sauce, monosodium glutamate, and red pepper. Simmer for twenty minutes. Taste for seasoning and correct if necessary. Serve very hot.

MISO SOUP WITH RADISH AND BURDOCK ROOT

6 cups *dashi* or chicken stock	3 oz burdock root
6 oz red bean paste, *aka-miso*	1 spring onion
6 oz Japanese radish, *daikon*	Monosodium glutamate

Peel the radish and cut into ¾-inch cubes. Scrape the burdock with the back of a knife, and cut into pieces about ¼ inch in diameter and 1 inch long. Put in cold water to prevent discoloration. Bring the stock to the boil and add the radish and burdock root and cook until tender. Mix the bean paste with a little of the hot soup and then return the stock and *miso* mixture to the saucepan. Mix well and bring to the boil. Add the spring onion, cut diagonally into ¼-inch widths, and a dash of monosodium glutamate and serve immediately.

SATSUMA-JIRU (*Miso Soup with Chicken and Vegetables*)

8 cups water	4 or 5 dried mushrooms
1 lb chicken	6 oz red bean paste, *aka-miso*
1 teaspoon salt	1 spring onion
1 small carrot	Monosodium glutamate
4 oz burdock root	*Shichimi* pepper (optional)
8 oz Japanese radish, *daikon*	

Put the chicken and water into a large saucepan with the salt and bring to the boil. Reduce heat and simmer for about one hour, until the chicken is very tender. Skim the surface occasionally to clear away the residue. Strain the stock into a clean saucepan, removing any fat, and when the chicken is cool enough to handle remove the meat from the bones and reserve. Soak the dried mushrooms in water until soft, trim away any tough stems and cut into cubes. Reserve the water in which the mushrooms soaked. Clean the carrot, burdock root and radish, and cut into cubes of the same size. Add all the vegetables and the reserved mushroom liquid to the broth and cook until tender. Add a dash of monosodium glutamate, taste for seasoning and add more salt if necessary, remembering that the *miso* paste is salty. Add a little of the hot broth to the *miso* and mix well, then return the mixture to the soup, stirring briskly. Bring to the boil and add the spring onion, chopped finely, and the chicken. Serve at once. If available, have *shichimi* pepper on the table to be used as desired.

MISO SOUP WITH FRIED BEAN CURD

6 cups *dashi* or chicken broth
6 oz red bean paste, *aka-miso*
2 pieces fried bean curd, *aburage*

2 spring onions
Monosodium glutamate

Pour boiling water over the fried bean curd in order to remove the excess oil and cut into strips ¼ inch wide. Cut the spring onions into quarters lengthwise, then into 1-inch pieces. Put the stock and the fried bean curd into a saucepan and bring to the boil. Remove a little of the hot stock and mix with the bean paste, then return the mixture to the saucepan. Bring to the boil again, add a dash of monosodium glutamate and the spring onion, and serve immediately.

MISO SOUP WITH FISH DUMPLINGS

6 oz filleted white fish
½ teaspoon salt
2 tablespoons cornflour
4 tablespoons flour
2 egg whites
2 teaspoons *sake*

6 cups *dashi* or chicken stock
6 oz red bean paste, *aka-miso*
12 small white mushrooms
1 spring onion, or 1 bunch trefoil
    leaves, *mitsuba*

Make the fish dumplings by pounding the fish to a paste in a *suribachi* or in a mortar. Add a pinch of salt, the cornflour and flour alternately with the egg whites and *sake* and mix until it is a good, stiff paste. Form the mixture into tiny balls. Cook by dropping into boiling water and removing when they rise to the surface. Drain and reserve.

Heat the stock and when it comes to the boil add a little of it to the bean paste and mix well. Return the bean paste mixture to the saucepan and add the fish dumplings and the mushrooms, sliced thin. Bring to the boil again. Add the spring onion, sliced diagonally into ¼-inch widths, or the trefoil greens and serve immediately.

MISO SOUP WITH PORK, BEAN SPROUTS, AND BURDOCK ROOT

6 cups *dashi* or chicken stock	1 oz bean sprouts
4 oz lean pork	6 oz red bean paste, *aka-miso*
3 oz burdock root	Monosodium glutamate

Cut the pork into ½-inch cubes. Scrape the burdock root with the back of a knife and cut into julienne style. Wash the bean sprouts. Bring the *dashi* or chicken stock to the boil in a large saucepan and add the pork and burdock root. Simmer until tender. Mix the bean paste with a little of the hot broth and then return the mixture to the saucepan. Stir briskly. Bring to the boil and add the bean sprouts and a dash of monosodium glutamate. Cook for one or two minutes longer, and serve.

MISO SOUP WITH BEAN CURD

6 cups *dashi*	2 spring onions
6 oz red bean paste, *aka-miso*	1 small carrot
1 piece of bean curd, *tōfu*	Monosodium glutamate

Cut the carrot into thin slices. Cut the spring onions diagonally into ¼-inch widths. Cut the bean curd into 1-inch squares. Bring the *dashi* to the boil, add the carrots and cook until tender. Remove a little of the hot stock and mix it with the bean paste, then return the mixture to the saucepan. Mix well. Add the bean curd carefully and bring to the boil again. Add the spring onions, simmer for only a few seconds, and serve immediately.

MISO SOUP WITH PORK AND SPINACH

6 cups water	8 oz fresh spinach
1 lb lean pork	1 spring onion
1 teaspoon salt	1-inch piece of fresh ginger root
Monosodium glutamate	6 oz red bean paste, *aka-miso*

Cut the pork into ½-inch cubes and put into the water with the salt and monosodium glutamate. Bring to the boil and simmer until done, about five minutes. Wash the spinach and coarsely cut into 1-inch lengths. Mix a little of the hot broth with the *miso* paste, return it to the soup and mix well. Add the spinach and bring to the boil. Add the ginger root, grated, and the onion, minced, and serve immediately.

MISO SOUP WITH PORK AND WATERCRESS

Substitute one large bunch of watercress for the spinach and proceed as above.

RICE AND NOODLES

The Japanese language has several different words meaning rice, of which the most stately is *gohan* or 'honourable food'. It is a sad commentary on the way things are going that among the younger generation the word is used much less often than *raisu*, the nearest Japanese phonetic equivalent of the English word. However, whether it takes the form of *gohan* in an elegant bowl or *raisu* dumped in a heap on a plain white canteen plate, plain boiled rice is still the staple food of Japan, and is used as a constituent of innumerable more complex dishes.

Noodles are probably the next most widespread single family of foodstuffs, and are positively Italian in their variety. Though a later development than rice, noodles have formed an important part of the Japanese diet for centuries, and are very much easier to eat with chopsticks than might be imagined. Almost every sizeable railway station has its *udon* stand, and travellers down a bowl of *udon* in the same unthinking way that westerners may eat a bar of chocolate, just to pass the time. Noodles come especially into their own on New Year's Eve, when it is customary to make a special point of eating them in some form or another. This is because their elongated shape is regarded as symbolic of, and therefore conducive to, longevity.

PLAIN BOILED RICE

The Japanese cook is judged by her skill in boiling rice in the way a western cook is judged by her dexterity in making an omelet. Allow ½ cup uncooked rice per person. Thoroughly wash the rice under cold running water, letting it drain through the rice until it runs clear. Put the rice in a colander and let it drain for an hour before cooking.

The amount of water used in the cooking is difficult to gauge. Really skilled Japanese cooks vary the amount of water in accordance with the season of the year and the time the rice was harvested. Even for those of us less skilled it is worth noting that European and American rice, grown in dry fields, absorbs more water than Asian rice, grown in flooded fields. As a rough guide use 1⅓ cups water for 1 cup Asian rice and 1¾ cups water for 1 cup European or American rice. With a little practice you should be able to tell how much water is suitable for your climate and your rice.

Put the rice and water together in a heavy-bottomed saucepan and cover with a heavy, well-fitting lid. Bring to the boil quickly, lower heat and let the contents simmer quietly for twenty minutes or until the water is absorbed. Then turn up the heat high for twenty to thirty seconds, leaving the lid on, and remove from the fire. Let the rice stand for ten minutes before serving. This final steaming in the retained heat helps to fluff up the rice. Serve in individual rice bowls.

BOILED RICE WITH GREEN PEAS

3 cups raw rice	3½ to 4½ cups water
1 cup cooked peas	Salt

Boil rice as in the preceding recipe. Cook the peas separately in salted

water, drain and keep warm. Just before serving carefully work the peas
into the rice with a fork or with chopsticks so that the rice does not
become sticky or lumpy. Serve hot.

TAKENOKO MESHI *(Rice and Bamboo Shoots)*

3 cups raw rice	1½ tablespoons *sake*
1 lb bamboo shoots	1½ tablespoons sugar
1 cup *dashi* or chicken stock	½ teaspoon salt
1½ tablespoons light soy sauce	Monosodium glutamate

Wash the rice well and drain for one hour before cooking. Cut the bamboo shoots into narrow strips, add to the *dashi* or chicken broth and boil
gently until tender. Remove the bamboo shoots from the broth and
keep warm. Into the soup put the soy sauce, *sake*, sugar and salt, and
enough water to bring the total volume to 3¼ to 3¾ cups (see recipe for
Plain Boiled Rice). Add the rice and mix well. Bring rapidly to the boil,
cover with a well-fitting lid, turn down the fire and simmer until the
rice is just tender and has absorbed all the stock. Turn up the heat for
twenty to thirty seconds, then remove from the fire. Add the bamboo
shoots, working them gently into the rice with a fork or chopsticks.
Cover again and let stand for five or ten minutes before serving.

KURIGOHAN *(Rice and Chestnuts)*

3 cups raw rice	1½ cups chopped chestnuts
3¼ to 3¾ cups water	1½ teaspoons salt
2 tablespoons *sake*	

Wash the rice carefully and drain for one hour before cooking. Either
fresh or tinned chestnuts may be used. If fresh, shell and remove the
skins carefully. Cut into thirds and soak for thirty minutes in cold
water. Put the rice, water, *sake*, salt, and chestnuts into a heavy-
bottomed saucepan. Cover tightly, bring to the boil and reduce heat to
a simmer. Cook for fifteen to twenty minutes or until the water is
absorbed. Turn up the heat for twenty to thirty seconds and then remove
from the fire. Let stand for ten minutes before serving.

GOMOKU MESHI (Garnished Rice)

3 cups raw rice
1½ oz burdock root
3 oz carrot
1½ oz fried bean curd, *aburage*
2 oz *konnyaku*
1¼ cups *dashi* or chicken broth

3 tablespoons light soy sauce
4 tablespoons *sake*
2 oz boned chicken
2 teaspoons light soy sauce
2–2½ cups water

One hour before cooking wash the rice thoroughly and drain in a colander. Scrape the burdock root with the back of a knife to remove the
skin, and grate on a large-holed grater into lengths of 1 to 1½ inches.
Drop into cold water to prevent discoloration. Cut the carrot into
julienne strips 1½ inches in length. Drop the *aburage* into boiling water
and let stand for five minutes to remove some of the oil, then cut into
julienne strips. Wash the *konnyaku*, salt slightly, and cut into julienne
strips. Cut the boned chicken obliquely into thin strips and sprinkle
over it two teaspoons light soy sauce.

Put the drained carrots, burdock root, *konnyaku* and *aburage* into a
saucepan with the *dashi* or chicken broth, the soy sauce and *sake*.
Simmer for ten minutes, and then drain the vegetables. Add enough
water to the broth to make 3½ to 4 cups liquid in all. Into a heavy-
bottomed saucepan put the rice, liquid, vegetables and chicken, and
cover. Bring to the boil, reduce heat, and simmer for twenty to twenty-
five minutes. (The addition of the soy sauce may increase the cooking
time slightly.) Remove from the fire and let stand for ten minutes with
the lid on before serving.

MATSUTAKE GOHAN (Rice and Mushrooms)

3 cups raw rice
3¼ to 3¾ cups water
1 piece kelp, *kombu* seaweed
   (optional)
6 oz *matsutake* mushrooms or
   fresh button mushrooms

3 tablespoons light soy sauce
2 tablespoons *sake*
½ teaspoon salt

Wash the rice well and drain for one hour before cooking. Wash the
mushrooms in cold water, trim away any tough stems and cut into thin
slices. Put the drained rice, the piece of kelp if available, soy sauce, *sake*,

and water into a heavy-bottomed saucepan and bring quickly to the boil. Remove the kelp immediately (it is used only for flavouring the water). Add the mushrooms and salt, and cover. Bring to the boil again, reduce heat to a simmer and cook for fifteen to twenty minutes or until the water has been absorbed. Turn up the heat for twenty to thirty seconds, then remove from the fire and let stand for ten minutes before serving.

SHŌGA-MESHI (Rice and Ginger)

3 cups raw rice
3¼ to 3¾ cups water
3 tablespoons light soy sauce
2 tablespoons *sake*

1 2-inch piece of fresh ginger root
1 3-inch piece of kelp, *kombu* seaweed (optional)

Wash the rice well and drain for one hour before cooking. Wash the ginger root and scrape its surface or cut away stained bits if necessary. Slice into thin, matchlike sticks and soak in cold water for thirty minutes. Put the rice, water, soy sauce, *sake*, and kelp, if available, into a heavy-bottomed saucepan. Bring to the boil quickly and remove the piece of kelp immediately (it is used only for flavouring the water). Drain the ginger, add to the rice and cover. Bring to the boil again, reduce heat to a simmer and continue to cook until the water is absorbed, about twenty minutes. Turn up the heat for twenty to thirty seconds, remove from the fire and let stand for ten minutes before serving. This mixture of rice and ginger has a light, fresh taste and is a good summer dish.

RICE WITH CHICKEN AND VEGETABLES

3 cups raw rice
4 oz boned chicken
3 dried mushrooms or 5 to 6
   fresh mushrooms
2 oz carrot

3 tablespoons light soy sauce
2 tablespoons *sake*
3¼ to 3¾ cups water
2 pieces laver seaweed, *nori*
   (optional)

Wash the rice thoroughly and let drain for one hour in a colander. Cut the chicken into thin strips. Cut both the carrot and the mushrooms into julienne style pieces. (If dried mushrooms are used, soak in cold water until soft.) Put the carrots, mushrooms, chicken, *sake*, and soy sauce in a saucepan. Bring quickly to the boil, remove from the heat and let the vegetables and chicken marinate in the remaining liquid until the rice is ready to cook.

Put the drained rice, the water and the marinated vegetables and chicken into a heavy-bottomed saucepan. Cover, bring quickly to the boil, reduce heat and simmer for fifteen to twenty minutes. Remove from the heat and let stand for ten minutes without taking off the lid. Turn out on to a serving dish or into individual rice bowls. If available, serve with a garnish of laver seaweed. Pass each piece of seaweed back and forth over a gas flame for a few moments until thoroughly dry and crisp, then crumble into pieces and sprinkle over the rice.

KAKIMESHI (Rice and Oysters)

3 cups raw rice	2 tablespoons light soy sauce
3¼ to 3¾ cups water	½ lb small oysters
2 tablespoons *sake*	1 teaspoon salt
1 3-inch piece of kelp, *kombu* seaweed (optional)	

Wash the rice well and drain for one hour before cooking. Wash the oysters in cold, salted water and drain. Put the rice, water, soy sauce, *sake*, and kelp, if available, into a heavy-bottomed saucepan and bring to the boil. Remove the piece of kelp which is used only for seasoning and add half the oysters. Cover tightly, bring to the boil again and reduce heat to a simmer. Cook for fifteen to twenty minutes or until the water is absorbed. Turn up the heat for twenty to thirty seconds, then remove from the fire. Add the remaining oysters, working them gently into the rice with chopsticks or a fork. Re-cover and let stand for ten minutes before serving.

NORI-CHAZUKE (Rice, Tea, and Seaweed)

An odd combination, but one which the Japanese are fond of; it is thought to be a capital way of finishing off an evening of drinking (serves one).

1½ cups hot cooked rice	1 cup hot *ocha*, Japanese tea
1 sheet laver seaweed, *nori*	

Place the rice in a bowl, pour the tea over it and crumble over the top a piece of *nori* which has been toasted by passing it back and forth over a gas flame or a burner. Serve immediately.

A variation of this is made by using soup stock in place of tea.

1 cup *dashi* or well-seasoned chicken broth	½ oz salt
	1 teaspoon light soy sauce
½ oz powdered Japanese horseradish, *wasabi*	Monosodium glutamate

Mix the horseradish to a paste with a little water. Put all the ingredients in a saucepan and bring to the boil. Simmer for ten minutes and pour over the rice.

SUSHI

The *sushiya*, or sushi shop, plays in Japan a role curiously similar to that of the pub in England, and its atmosphere is equally relaxed and informal. There are little booths or tables where the effete can sit and eat their prepared lacquer boxes of the ambrosia. The true enthusiast, however, sits up at the bar on a high stool, gossiping to the master and his assistants, and ordering his *sushi* a pair at a time, selecting his preferred kind of fish or other delicacy from the refrigerated display in front of him, and washing the *sushi* down with plenty of green tea or beer. There is a whole jargon associated with this type of *sushi*, which is called *nigiri* or hand-made, and consists of little patties of rice savoured with vinegar surmounted by strips (or slabs in expensive *sushiya*) of raw fish, octopus, squid, a kind of omelet and a variety of other tidbits. *Nigiri-zushi*, though it is the undisputed head of the family, is only one of many varieties of dish utilizing the principle of uniting the flavours of cold dressed rice and various kinds of fish and egg, and even if one cannot hope to capture in one's home the authentic *sushiya* atmosphere, one can without too much difficulty produce many varieties of this exotic and quite splendid Japanese speciality.

COOKING RICE FOR SUSHI

The preparation of the rice for *sushi* is said to be the key to its success or failure, and the *aficionado* always begins with a mild-flavoured piece of egg *sushi* in order to taste the quality of the rice.

3 cups raw rice	$\frac{1}{3}$ cup vinegar
3$\frac{1}{4}$ to 3$\frac{3}{4}$ cups water	2 tablespoons sugar
1 5-inch piece of kelp, *kombu*	1$\frac{1}{2}$ teaspoons salt
seaweed (optional)	Monosodium glutamate

Wash the rice thoroughly and let it drain for one hour before cooking. Put the rice, water, and the kelp, if available, into a heavy-bottomed saucepan and bring to the boil. Remove the kelp at this point or it will flavour the rice too strongly. Cover the saucepan again, and simmer the rice for fifteen to twenty minutes or until it is just tender. Rice cooked for *sushi* should be slightly harder in texture than for other dishes. Remove from the fire and let it stand covered for ten minutes.

Put the vinegar, sugar, salt, and a dash of monosodium glutamate into a small saucepan, bring to the boil and remove from the fire. Put the hot rice into a large bowl, wooden if possible. Pour the vinegar mixture evenly over the surface of the rice, mixing it into the rice with quick, cutting strokes. Fan the rice at the same time. This fanning, which cools the rice quickly, produces the glossy sheen prized in a good *sushi* base.

NIGIRI-ZUSHI

Prepared *sushi* rice	2 oz Japanese horseradish, *wasabi*
6 prawns	1 fresh ginger root, cleaned and
1 lb assorted fresh fish (tuna,	thinly sliced
bream, abalone, squid,	
octopus, etc)	

Dip the prawns into boiling water until they turn pink. They should be only barely cooked. Remove the shells, leaving the tail section intact. Slit along the underside and open flat, making certain that the prawn is clean and de-veined. The other kinds of fish are eaten raw. Fillet the fish and cut it carefully and neatly into rectangular pieces 2 inches by 1$\frac{1}{2}$ inches and $\frac{1}{4}$ inch. The squid and octopus, if extremely fresh, are also eaten raw, but they may be sliced into pieces the same size as the other fish and briefly dipped into boiling water if preferred. Grate the fresh horseradish or mix the powdered horseradish to a paste with a little water and allow to stand for a few minutes.

Prepare the *sushi* rice according to the previous recipe. In the right hand take about two tablespoons of the *sushi* rice and shape it into an oblong about 2 inches by 1 inch. The fillets of fish should just droop over the ends of the rice to be most attractive. With the left hand put a dab of the horseradish on the rice, then a piece of the fish. Horseradish is not used with the shrimp. Serve the *sushi* soon after its is made, with condiments of soy sauce, into which an end of the *sushi* is dipped, and sliced, fresh ginger, a thin slice being put on pieces as desired. Eat either with the fingers or with chopsticks.

CHIRASHIZUSHI

This is a kind of rice salad in which various ingredients are mixed into the prepared *sushi* rice. Do not limit yourself to the ingredients listed below, but substitute and add ingredients with a free hand.

Prepared *sushi* rice	1 oz lotus root, *renkon*
1 oz dried gourd shavings, *kampyō*	2 eggs
½ small carrot	Sugar
3 or 4 dried mushrooms	Light soy sauce
2 oz tinned shrimp	Vinegar
1 oz bamboo shoots	Monosodium glutamate
1 oz green peas	

Prepare the *sushi* rice according to the recipe on page 54. Soak the dried gourd shavings and dried mushrooms in water for twenty minutes or until soft. Slice into narrow pieces. Slice the carrot into thin rounds or matchsticks and boil in a little salted water, two tablespoons soy sauce and one teaspoon sugar until tender and well-flavoured. Cut the bamboo into thin slices and cook in the same way as the carrot. Drain the shrimp. Boil the peas in salted water until tender. Peel the lotus root and soak it in water for about ten minutes. Slice into thin rounds. Put in fresh water and boil with one tablespoon vinegar until tender but still crisp. Beat the eggs, add a dash of salt, monosodium glutamate and half teaspoon sugar and cook in a thin omelet. Slice the omelet into narrow pieces, about the same size as the other vegetables. Mix all the ingredients carefully into the rice and decorate the top with a few pieces of the lotus root and the omelet strips and some green peas.

Other ingredients which can be added to *chirashizushi* are small snow peas, green beans, clams, raw tuna, *chirimen-jako* or small cooked fish, and *kōyadōfu* or dried bean curd.

OSHI-ZUSHI (*Pressed Sushi*)

This type of *sushi* is pressed in special wooden moulds called *oshiwaku*, but it can be made perfectly well in an ordinary cake tin with a removable bottom. Pressed *sushi* is extremely attractive and is ideal as an *hors-d'oeuvre* with drinks or for a picnic lunch. A variety of toppings can be used such as raw fish, thinly slice cooked chicken, smoked salmon, etc; we have chosen ham, prawns, and omelet.

Prepared *sushi* rice (*see* page 54)	2 tablespoons *mirin* wine
3 dried mushrooms	3 slices roast ham
½ small cucumber	6 prawns
1 small carrot	Salt
1 egg	Monosodium glutamate
2 tablespoons dark soy sauce	2 teaspoons Japanese horseradish,
1 tablespoon sugar	*wasabi*

Soak the mushrooms in warm water for fifteen minutes or until soft. Scrape the carrot and cut into matchlike sticks 1½ inches long. Remove the mushrooms from the water and slice into narrow lengths. Into a small saucepan put half cup of the water in which the mushrooms were soaked, the soy sauce, *mirin*, sugar, and a dash of monosodium glutamate. Add the mushrooms and carrots and simmer for about five minutes or until well-flavoured. Drain away the liquid and put aside the carrots and mushrooms to cool. Cut the cucumber without peeling into thin, diagonal slices, then cut the slices into narrow lengths. Salt and let stand for a few minutes.

Beat the egg, add a dash of salt and monosodium glutamate and a pinch of sugar. Heat a little oil in a frying pan and fry the egg in a thin omelet, being careful that it does not turn brown. Remove and reserve. Immerse the prawns in boiling salted water until they turn pink. Remove, drain and when cool enough to handle remove shells, tails and carefully clean and de-vein. Cut the prawns lengthwise into halves.

Oil a square cake tin with a removable bottom. Pack the *sushi* rice into the tin about half way up the sides and press down evenly with your finger tips. It is useful to keep your fingers wet when working with *sushi* rice. Top with a layer of the mushrooms, carrots, and cucumbers. If the mushrooms contain a great deal of moisture squeeze them to remove most of it. Put the remaining rice on top of the vegetables and press down evenly. Mix the powdered horseradish with a little cold water to a smooth paste and spread evenly over the surface of the rice.

Arrange the prawns, ham, and omelet decoratively on top of the rice, remembering that it will be cut into squares. Cover the top with a sheet of waxed paper, put another pan of the same size on top of the *sushi* and weight it down with a heavy saucepan or other weight. Leave the *sushi* weighted for fifteen minutes. Remove the weights and wax paper, run a knife around the edge of the *sushi* and remove the sides of the cake tin. With a sharp, wet knife cut the *sushi* into pieces, arrange on a platter and serve. Have a little soy sauce available for guests to sprinkle on each piece as it is eaten, if they so desire.

ONIGIRI

These extremely simple rice balls are an invariable element of the *bento*, those extremely elegant laquered lunch boxes which not only accompany families on picnics but are also an important part of the pleasure of attending *kabuki*, where they are brought out and eaten in the interval. So common are they that the most popular type of *bento* is called *makunouchi* or 'during the intermission'.

6 cups cooked rice	2 teaspoons salt
2 tablespoons black sesame seeds	6 slices smoked salmon or raw tuna

Cook the rice according to the recipe for Plain Boiled Rice. Make the balls while the rice is still hot. Cut the salmon or tuna into 1-inch lengths, no more than ¼ inch in diameter. Wet your hands and take a handful of rice. Press two or three pieces of fish into the centre and mould the rice around it, forming a cylinder about 2 inches long and 1 inch in diameter. Form cylinders from the remaining rice and fish, keeping your hands wet so that the rice does not cling to them. Roast the sesame seeds with the salt in a dry frying pan, stirring to prevent burning, until the seeds begin to jump. Remove from the fire and sprinkle over the rice balls. Other fish, meat, cooked vegetables, or pickles may be substituted for the salmon or, indeed, *onigiri* may be made plain without enclosing any ingredients. They are always eaten at room temperature.

NORIMAKI

This type of *sushi* is rolled into a cylindrical shape with a covering of seaweed and an inner core of fish, mushroom, egg, or various other ingredients.

Prepared *sushi* rice (*see* page 54)
8–10 sheets of laver seaweed, *nori*
1–2 dried mushrooms
1 oz dried gourd shavings, *kampyō* (optional)
2 oz raw tuna
½ small cucumber

2 eggs
½ cup water or *dashi* broth
3 tablespoons soy sauce
1 tablespoon sugar
1 tablespoon *mirin*
Monosodium glutamate

Soak the mushrooms and dried gourd shavings in cold water for about twenty minutes or until soft. Slice into long, thin pieces. Put into a small saucepan with the water or broth, soy sauce, sugar and *mirin* and cook until the liquid is almost absorbed and the vegetables well-flavoured. Drain and reserve. The tuna is eaten raw. Slice it into thin sticks about ¼ inch in diameter and 3 to 4 inches long. Beat the eggs, add a pinch of salt and monosodium glutamate, and fry in a thin omelet. Cut this into thin strips as well. Cut the cucumber into sticks the same size as the tuna.

Toast the sheets of seaweed by passing them back and forth over a flame for a few moments until thoroughly crisp. Place one sheet of the seaweed on top of a *sudare* or bamboo mat (a bamboo table mat may be substituted). Spread one cup of the *sushi* rice evenly over the bottom two-thirds of the sheet of seaweed. Place across the centre of the rice a strand of the gourd shavings and the mushroom; a piece of tuna lightly dabbed with horseradish; strands of the omelet; or sticks of the cucumber. Roll the *sushi* in the bamboo mat, pressing firmly so that the materials adhere to each other in a neat cylinder. Remove the bamboo roll and with a sharp knife slice the *norimaki* into inch-wide slices. If the knife is wiped with a clean, damp cloth after each cut the slices will be neater. Repeat the process until all the rice and fillings have been used.

INARIZUSHI

These small bags of fried bean curd containing *sushi* rice are extremely popular for picnics and outings of all kinds and are the Japanese equivalent of a pack of ham sandwiches. Many westerners will not share the Japanese devotion to fried bean curd, but many others, once they get over its slightly unprepossessing appearance, will find it extremely tasty.

Prepared *sushi* rice (*see* page 54)   2 tablespoons sugar
10 sheets *aburage*, fried bean curd   1 tablespoon *sake*
⅔cup *dashi* broth   ¼ teaspoon monosodium glutamate
3 tablespoons soy sauce   2 teaspoons white sesame seeds

Pour a kettle of boiling water over the bean curd in order to cleanse it of excess oil. Cut the squares in halves and pull open the centre of the pieces, making bags of them. Put the *dashi*, soy sauce, sugar, *sake*, and monosodium glutamate in a saucepan and bring to the boil. Add the bean curd bags and simmer for ten to fifteen minutes, until the liquid has been almost absorbed and the bean curd is well flavoured. Remove from the fire, drain well and cool. Press out any remaining liquid with a clean cloth.

Heat the sesame seeds in a dry frying pan until they begin to jump, stirring constantly to prevent them from burning. Add the toasted sesame seeds to the *sushi* rice, mixing until they are evenly distributed through the rice. Fill the bean curd bags with the prepared *sushi* rice and roll the top of the bean curd over the rice to enclose it. Arrange on a platter and serve. Instead of, or in addition to, the sesame seeds, small pieces of mushroom, carrot, dried gourd or other vegetables cooked in the same liquid as the bean curd can be added to the rice before filling the bags.

DONBURI

The word *donburi* in Japanese means a large, china bowl, but the name of the bowl has come to be attached to the kind of food which so frequently goes into it, hot rice with various toppings, over which is poured a sauce. Its virtues of economy and ease of preparation make it a favourite lunch-time snack. Japanese housewives use it as a means of using up leftovers, as virtually any meat, fish, or vegetable can be used for the topping.

OYAKO DONBURI (*Parent and Child Donburi*)

3 cups raw rice
12 oz boned chicken
2 spring onions
12 eggs

3 cups *dashi* or chicken broth
¾ cup light soy sauce
¾ cup *mirin*

Boil the rice according to the basic recipe on page 48. Cut the chicken into cubes about ½ inch in diameter. Cut the spring onions, including the green tops, into ¼-inch slices. Put the *dashi* or chicken broth into a saucepan, add the soy sauce and the *mirin*. Heat, and when it comes to the boil add the chicken. Simmer for five minutes, add the spring onions and cook for one minute longer. Taste for seasoning and correct if necessary.

Break the eggs into a large bowl and beat well. Bring the soup stock to the boil again, and gently but all at once pour in the eggs. Continue heating until the mixture begins to boil around the edge of the pan. Turn the fire down as low as possible and put on a lid. After three minutes turn off the fire. The eggs will have coagulated into a soft mass resembling scrambled eggs. Put the rice into individual bowls, and with a ladle spoon the egg and soup mixture over the top of the rice. Decorate with a little chopped parsley, a few green peas or chopped green onions. Serve immediately.

KITSUNE DONBURI (Bean Curd Donburi)

3 cups raw rice
3 sheets *aburage*, fried bean curd
3 spring onions
3 cups *dashi* or chicken broth

¾ cup light soy sauce
¾ cup *mirin* wine
Monosodium glutamate

Boil the rice according to the basic recipe on page 48. Dip the pieces of bean curd into boiling water in order to remove some of their oil. Cut them into slices 1½ inches long and ½ inch wide. Put together with the *dashi*, soy sauce, *mirin* and a dash of monosodium glutamate into a saucepan and simmer for ten minutes. Cut the spring onions diagonally into pieces about ¼ inch wide. Add them to the simmering soup and cook for one minute longer. Put the rice into individual rice bowls and pour the hot soup over the top. *Kitsune donburi* is usually not decorated with any greenery.

KATSUDON (Cutlet Donburi)

This recipe is useful for using up those pieces of pork or lamb cutlet left from the night before.

1 large white onion
1 lb left-over pork or lamb cutlets
3 cups *dashi* or chicken stock

½ cup soy light sauce
¾ cup *mirin*
3 cups raw rice

Boil the rice according to the basic recipe on page 48. Pour the *dashi* or chicken stock, the soy sauce, and the *mirin* into a saucepan and bring to the boil. Cut the onion into slices, separate the rings and cut into lengths of about 1½ inches. Add the onions to the boiling stock and cook until tender, about five minutes. Cut the meat into ½-inch widths. Drop into the boiling soup and cook until the meat is just heated through. Put the hot cooked rice into individual bowls, arrange the pieces of meat on top and spoon the broth and onions over them. Serve immediately.

TENDON

Tendon is an abbreviated form of *tempura donburi*. Usually left-over *tempura* is used for this dish, and a piece of fried fish might well be substituted.

3 cups raw rice
12 pieces *tempura*, preferably
    prawn (*see* page 86)
3 cups *dashi* or chicken stock

¾ cup light soy sauce
¾ cup *mirin*
3 spring onions
Shichimi pepper (optional)

Boil the rice according to the basic recipe on page 48. Heat the *dashi* or chicken stock, the soy sauce, and the *mirin* in a saucepan until it comes to the boil. Meanwhile warm the *tempura* in the oven. Put the rice into individual bowls, put two pieces of *tempura* on each dish of rice and pour the boiling sauce over it all. *Tendon* may be garnished with chopped spring onions or with *shichimi* pepper. Serve immediately.

UNAGI DONBURI (*Eel Donburi*)

3 cups raw rice
6 pieces grilled eel

½ cup dark soy sauce
1 cup *mirin*

Boil the rice according to the basic recipe on page 48. Grill the eel according to the recipe on page 100, reserving the left-over marinade. Put the hot cooked rice into individual bowls, top with a piece of the hot grilled eel and pour the remaining marinade, heated to boiling point, over the top. Serve immediately.

YAKITORI DONBURI (*Fried Chicken Donburi*)

3 cups raw rice
1 frying chicken
¾ cup *mirin*
¾ cup light soy sauce
2 teaspoons grated garlic

3 tablespoons oil
3 cups *dashi* or chicken stock
1½ tablespoons sugar
½ cup chopped parsley or green
    peas

Boil the rice. Prepare a marinade of the *mirin*, the soy sauce and the garlic. Cut the chicken into pieces and let it stand in this mixture for twenty minutes. Heat the oil in a frying pan. Drain and dry the chicken, and fry it until done. When cool enough to handle cut the meat off the bones in strips about 1½ inches long and ½ inch wide. Reserve and keep warm. Put the *dashi* or chicken stock, the sugar, and the remaining marinade in a saucepan and bring to the boil. Distribute the hot rice among six bowls, arrange the chicken on top and pour the hot broth over it all. The top may be decorated with a little chopped parsley or a few green peas. Serve immediately.

Noodles

The Japanese rejoice in many types and sizes of noodles, from the brown buckwheat variety called *soba* through the fine, white, shining lengths of *sōmen* to the product called *shirataki* made from a vegetable root. They are eaten in a variety of ways – in soups, in casseroles, fried and even, on hot muggy summer days, ice cold. Here are a few of the more popular recipes.

HOW TO COOK DRIED NOODLES

All the forms of dried noodles – *soba, udon, sōmen, and hiyamugi* – are boiled in approximately the same way. If the package you buy contains instructions follow them; if not, use the following method. In a large saucepan bring enough water to the boil to cover the noodles well. When it is boiling hard add the noodles and stir slowly. Let the water come to a boil again, then add one cup cold water. Bring to the boil a second time (purists insist that cold water be added twice more, but you can be judge of whether this is necessary) and continue to cook until the noodles are tender. Do not overcook or they will become mushy. Drain in a colander and rinse under running, cold water. Cold cooked noodles may be re-heated easily by putting them in a colander and pouring a kettle of boiling water over them.

KAKEJIRU (Soup Stock for Noodles)

The soup stock used in the preparation of noodle dishes is of the utmost importance since it determines the flavour of the entire dish. If the soup tastes insipid, so will the noodles.

6 cups *dashi* or chicken stock $\frac{1}{2}$ teaspoon salt
$\frac{1}{4}$ cup light soy sauce   Monosodium glutamate
$\frac{1}{4}$ cup *mirin*

Heat the *dashi* or chicken stock and taste for seasoning. Add the *mirin*, soy sauce, salt, and a dash of monosodium glutamate. Bring to the boil and taste again for seasoning, correcting if necessary. Simmer for ten minutes.

TSUKEJIRU DIPPING SAUCE

Tsukejiru contains the same seasonings as the *kakejiru* soup above, but in different proportions which results in a stronger, more savoury mixture used basically as a dipping sauce.

2 cups *dashi* or chicken stock ½ cup dark soy sauce
½ cup *mirin* Monosodium glutamate

Mix all ingredients in a small saucepan and bring to the boil. Taste for seasoning, correct if necessary and cool before using.

TEMPURA SOBA (*Tempura Buckwheat Noodles*)

The brown, lighter buckwheat noodles are the favourite combination with *tempura*, but *udon* or *lasagne* noodles may be substituted if desired.

1 lb dried *soba* noodles 6 cups *kakejiru* soup (*see* page 63)
12 pieces *tempura* (*see* page 86) *Shichimi* pepper if available
Lemon peel

Boil the *soba* according to the recipe on page 63. Drain, rinse in cold water and reserve. Prepare the *tempura* pieces (or substitute six small pieces of fried fish). Bring the *kakejiru* soup to the boil. Re-heat the *soba* by pouring a kettle of boiling water over them, drain and arrange in six warm bowls. Place the hot pieces of *tempura* or fried fish on top of the noodles and add the boiling soup. Decorate with thin slices of lemon peel. Serve immediately. If available, have on the table *shichimi* pepper to be added to taste.

GOMOKU-UDON (*Garnished Noodles*)

1 lb dried *udon* noodles or 6 portions fresh noodles (if not available substitute *lasagne* noodles) ½ lb raw spinach or
¾ lb lean pork chrysanthemum leaves
6–12 dried mushrooms 3 spring onions
¾ lb carrots 6 cups *kakejiru* soup (*see* page 63)

Cut the pork into thin slices or into bite-size cubes. Soak the dried mushrooms in cold water for about twenty minutes or until soft, and cut away the hard stems. Save the liquid in which the mushrooms were soaked and add it to the *kakejiru* soup. Scrape the carrot and cut it into thin slices. Slice the spring onions, including green tops, diagonally into ½-inch widths. Wash the spinach or chrysanthemum leaves carefully and cut off any tough stems on the spinach.

If using dried noodles cook according to the instructions on page 63. Drain, rinse, and reserve. Heat the *kakejiru* broth, add the pork, mushrooms and carrots and cook for five minutes. Put the spinach and spring onions into the broth and cook for a further minute. If using chrysanthemum leaves, they need only be dipped into the broth for twenty seconds or so. Re-heat the noodles by pouring a kettle of boiling water over them. Distribute the hot noodles among six large, warmed soup bowls and arrange the vegetables and pork on top. Pour the boiling soup over it all and serve immediately. If available, have on the table a container of *shichimi* pepper to be added as desired.

GOMOKU-SOBA (*Garnished Buckwheat Noodles*)

Substitute *soba* noodles for the *udon* noodles and proceed as in the above recipe.

TORI-NAMBA UDON (*Chicken and Noodles*)

1 lb dried *udon* noodles or 6 portions fresh noodles (substitute *lasagne* noodles if *udon* is not available)

1 lb boned chicken	Salt
3 spring onions	Pepper
6 cups *kakejiru* soup (*see* page 63)	*Shichimi* pepper, if available

Cook the noodles, drain and rinse in cold running water. Heat the *kakejiru* soup and taste for seasoning, correcting if necessary. Cut the chicken into bite-sized pieces and add to the soup, simmering for about five minutes. Slice the spring onions, including green tops, diagonally into ½-inch widths. Re-heat the noodles by pouring a kettle of hot water over them. Drain, and distribute the noodles among six large, heated

3

soup bowls. Add the spring onions to the simmering soup and cook for
thirty seconds longer. Ladle the soup, chicken and spring onions over
the top of the noodles and serve immediately. Have salt and pepper on
the table as well as *shichimi* pepper if it is available.

TORI-NAMBA SOBA (*Chicken and Buckwheat Noodles*)

Substitute *soba* noodles for the *udon* noodles and proceed as in the above
recipe.

KITSUNE UDON (*Fox Noodles*)

No one is quite sure why this dish came to be associated with the fox,
that animal so redolent of evil spirits and magic in Japanese folklore,
although some say it is because of his proverbial fondness for bean curd
(hence *Kitsune Donburi* on page 61).

1 lb dried *udon* noodles or 6 portions fresh noodles (if not available
  substitute *lasagne* noodles)

6 pieces fried bean curd, *aburage*	Monosodium glutamate
6 tablespoons soy sauce	3 spring onions
2 tablespoons *mirin*	6 cups *kakejiru* soup (*see* page 63)
1 tablespoon sugar	*Shichimi* pepper, if available
½ cup water or *dashi*	

Cook the noodles according to the recipe on page 63. Drain, rinse, and
reserve. Dip the pieces of fried bean curd into boiling water in order to
remove some of the excess oil, then slice into ½-inch widths. Put into a
saucepan with the water or *dashi*, soy sauce, *mirin*, sugar, and a dash of
monosodium glutamate. Simmer the bean curd in this mixture for ten
minutes or until it has absorbed most of the liquid. Cut the spring
onions diagonally, including green tops, into ½-inch widths. Heat the
kakejiru soup to the boiling point. Warm the noodles by pouring a
kettle of boiling water over them and drain well. Distribute them among
six large, warmed soup bowls. Put the spring onions into the simmering

kakejiru broth for thirty seconds. Arrange the pieces of fried bean curd on top of the noodles, then ladle the soup and spring onions over it all. Serve immediately. Have on the table *shichimi* pepper if available.

OSAKA KITSUNE UDON (*Fox Noodles, Osaka Style*)

This noodle dish is a speciality from the seaport of Osaka. It is virtually the same as the above recipe, but includes chicken and mushrooms.

1 lb dried *udon* noodles	Monosodium glutamate
6 pieces fried bean curd, *aburage*	¾ lb boned chicken
6 tablespoons soy sauce	6 dried mushrooms
2 tablespoons *mirin*	3 spring onions
1 tablespoon sugar	6 cups *kakejiru* soup (*see* page 63)
½ cup water or *dashi*	

Soak the mushrooms in water until soft and slice into ½-inch widths. Simmer the mushrooms with the bean curd in the mixture of water, soy sauce, *mirin*, and sugar. Cut the chicken into bite-size pieces. Add the chicken to the *kakejiru* soup and simmer until tender. Otherwise proceed as in the above recipe.

KITSUNE SOBA (*Fox Buckwheat Noodles*)

Substitute *soba* noodles for the *udon* noodles and proceed as in the previous recipe.

NABEYAKI UDON

This hearty noodle casserole is guaranteed to keep one warm on even the coldest day. In Japan each serving is prepared in an individual, oven-proof bowl, but if more convenient it can be prepared in a single large casserole.

1 lb dried *udon* noodles
6 cups *kakejiru* soup (*see* page 63)
6 pieces prawn *tempura* or 6 small
   pieces of fried fish
6 large fresh mushrooms
½ lb boned chicken

3 spring onions
1 6-inch piece of fish sausage,
   kamaboko (optional)
Small bunch of fresh spinach or
   chrysanthemum leaves

Cook the noodles according to the recipe on page 63. Drain, rinse with cold water and set aside. Fry the prawn *tempura*, using the recipe on page 86, or substitute small pieces of fried fish. Slice the chicken into pieces ½ inch thick and 1½ inches long. Cut the fish sausage into slices about ⅓ inch thick. Clean the mushrooms and remove any tough stems. Leave whole or, if extremely large, cut into halves. Wash the spinach or chrysanthemum leaves, removing any tough stems on the spinach. Cut the spring onions, including tops, into diagonal slices.

Heat the *kakejiru* soup and check for seasoning. Divide the noodles among six oven-proof bowls or put all the noodles into one large casserole. Arrange on top the chicken, mushrooms, and slices of *kamaboko*. Pour in the hot soup stock, cover and cook in a pre-heated moderate (Mark 5) oven for fifteen minutes. Remove the casserole from the oven and add the pieces of *tempura* or fried fish, and the spinach or chrysanthemum leaves. Cover again, and put in the oven for a further five minutes or until the *tempura* is heated through and the spinach tender. Serve immediately.

ZARU SOBA (*Chilled Buckwheat Noodles*)

Cold noodles at first seem an odd dish to the western palate, but it is an extremely refreshing one on a hot summer day.

1 lb dried *soba* noodles or 6
   portions fresh *soba*
3 sheets laver seaweed, *nori*

3 spring onions
1 2-inch piece of fresh ginger root
3 cups *tsukejiru* sauce (*see* page 64)

Boil the dried *soba* noodles according to the recipe on page 63, rinse in cold water and drain. Slice the spring onions, including tops, finely. Grate the ginger and put into a small bowl. Toast the seaweed by passing it back and forth over a gas flame or electric burner until thoroughly dry and crisp. Arrange the cold noodles on six plates. In Japan *zaru soba* is always served in square, bamboo boxes with a slatted bottom, but ordinary plates are fine so long as the noodles are well drained. Crumble the seaweed over the top as a garnish. If seaweed is not available, garnish with a few chopped onions. Give each person a separate container of about half a cup of the *tsukejiru* sauce into which he puts the grated ginger or chopped spring onions as desired. The noodles are dipped into the sauce before being eaten.

ZARU UDON (Chilled Noodles)

Substitute *udon* or *lasagne* noodles for the *soba* noodles and prepare as in the above recipe.

HIYASHI SŌMEN

This is another cold noodle dish, favoured in summer, this time using the extremely fine *sōmen* noodle.

1 lb dried *sōmen* noodles	Salt
6 dried mushrooms	Soy sauce
12 large prawns	1 lemon
3 spring onions	4 cups *tsukejiru* sauce (*see* page 64)

Boil the *sōmen* noodles according to the recipe on page 63. Rinse in cold water and drain. Clean, de-vein and shell the prawns, leaving the tail shells intact. Drop into boiling salted water for two or three minutes or until they become pink and firm. Remove and drain. Soak the dried mushrooms in cold water until soft. Remove stems and season with salt and a little soy sauce. Cut the spring onions, including green tops, into very thin slices. Arrange the well-drained *sōmen* noodles in six dishes and put two prawns, a mushroom, and a thin slice of lemon on top of each. Give each person a small bowl of *tsukejiru* sauce into which he adds the chopped spring onions to taste. Grated ginger root may be substituted for the onions if desired. The noodles are dipped into the sauce before eating.

HIYASHI GOMOKU-SOBA (Chilled Garnished Noodles)

1 lb dried *soba* noodles

6 slices cooked ham

1 cucumber

5–6 dried mushrooms

¼ cup *dashi* or water in which the mushrooms were soaked

2 tablespoons soy sauce

2 tablespoons *mirin* or sugar

3 eggs

½ teaspoon salt

2 cups *tsukejiru* sauce (*see* page 64)

Cook the noodles according to the recipe on page 63. Rinse well in cold water and chill. Soak the mushrooms in water until soft, remove the stems and cut into thin strips. Mix together in a small saucepan the *dashi* broth or a quarter cup of the water in which the mushrooms soaked, the soy sauce and *mirin* or sugar. Add the mushrooms and cook for five or ten minutes. Drain and cool the mushrooms. Cut the ham and cucumbers into strips the same size as the mushrooms. Beat the eggs, add the salt and fry in a thin omelet. Cut the omelet into strips the same size as the other ingredients. Put the chilled noodles into individual bowls and arrange carefully and attractively on top separate sections of the mushroom, ham, cucumber, and omelet strips. Pour the *tsukejiru* sauce over all and serve.

COOKING AT THE TABLE

As we pointed out earlier, in the case of most Japanese dishes it is vitally important for them to be eaten as soon as possible after they are cooked. This being so, the Japanese have developed to a high degree the art of diminishing the distance between the point of cooking and the point of consumption. Many specialized restaurants such as *tempuraya* place their customers at a long, or sometimes circular, bar behind which the cook plies his art, depositing smoking hot mouthfuls one at a time on absorbent paper in front of them. The customers thus enjoy a free show as well as having their meal cooked literally while they are eating it. A skilled *tempura* cook can, by a triumph of time and motion, keep up to ten or even more hungry customers simultaneously happy and occupied, without benefit of waiter or dishwasher.

The same sensible principle is combined with a proper sense of the social delights of eating in some of Japan's most famous dishes which are cooked over a portable gas ring placed in the centre of a low table round which the guests kneel or sit on cushions, helping themselves as the food becomes ready. At elegant restaurants, depending on the dish, a waitress will sometimes put in the raw materials and the guest's task is limited to helping himself. At a private party the hostess or other volunteer will probably see to the replenishment of the pot for *sukiyaki* or *mizudaki*, but the whole point of *shabu-shabu*, for example, is for the guests to do their own cooking as well as serving themselves.

A gas ring is easily the most effective source of heat, and an electric ring will only serve if it generates enough heat to bring the contents of a heavy pan or pot to frying or boiling point reasonably quickly.

In the section which follows we offer a number of recipes which can and should be cooked at the table in this happy co-operative spirit.

SUKIYAKI

2 lb beef	1 piece grilled bean curd,
10 spring onions	*yakidōfu* (about ¾ lb)
¾ lb *shirataki* noodles	6 eggs
1 large onion	Light soy sauce
½ lb chrysanthemum leaves	Sugar
1 lb fresh mushrooms	*Sake*
2 small bamboo shoots	

For the beef choose good-quality, well-marbled steak and have your butcher slice it into wafer-thin slices on a bacon cutting machine. Wash the vegetables. Cut the spring onions, green tops as well, diagonally into 2- to 3-inch lengths. Slice the onion into rings. If you use fresh bamboo shoots boil until just tender; if tinned, drain and slice into pieces ¼ inch thick. Drain the bean curd and cut into 1½-inch squares. Leave the mushrooms whole, removing the stems if they are tough. Drain the *shirataki* noodles. Arrange the meat and vegetables attractively on large platters.

Put a *sukiyaki* pan or a large, heavy frying pan over a portable cooking stove in the centre of the dining-table and melt a small piece of suet in it. When it is melted add some of the meat and spring onions. When the meat has slightly browned sprinkle both the beef and the spring onions lightly with sugar, then with soy sauce and *sake*. The liquid from the seasonings and the juices from the meat and vegetables should be enough to keep the ingredients from sticking to the pan. Serve from the frying pan as things become done, adding more vegetables and meat which continue to cook while the guests eat. Season to taste with the soy sauce, sugar and *sake*. Each guest helps himself to things as they become ready.

To eat *sukiyaki* each person breaks a raw egg into a bowl, beating it lightly with his chopsticks. The meat and vegetables are then dipped into the egg and eaten. When dealing with a piece of meat larger than one mouthful, it is quite good manners to bite a piece off while holding the remainder in the chopsticks. The usual accompaniment to *sukiyaki* is plain boiled rice.

CHICKEN SUKIYAKI

2 lb raw chicken, cut off the bone
Prepare as for the recipe above, but for the beef substitute chicken cut off the bone and into pieces about 1 inch by 3 inches by ½ inch.

SHABU-SHABU

2 lb steak
12 large mushrooms
12 spring onions
¼ head of Chinese cabbage
½ lb bamboo shoots
1 piece of grilled bean curd,
    yakidōfu (about ¾ lb)
1 oz Japanese horseradish, *wasabi*
2 quarts chicken stock

INGREDIENTS FOR SAUCE
3 oz white sesame seeds
1 cup *dashi* or chicken stock
½ cup light soy sauce
1½ tablespoons dark soy sauce
1 teaspoon sesame seed oil
½ teaspoon finely cut hot red
    peppers
1 tablespoon lemon juice or vinegar

First prepare the sauce. Put the sesame seeds in a dry, heavy frying pan and toast them, shaking and stirring the pan to prevent scorching. When the seeds begin to jump remove from the fire and crush in a *suribachi* or mortar, or put through a nut grinder. Add the soup stock, either hot or cold, stirring to prevent lumps forming. Add the other ingredients and blend well. This sauce will keep in the refrigerator for three or four days.

The beef should be good-quality, well-marbled steak cut on a slicing machine to the thinness of bacon. Wash the vegetables. Cut the spring onions, including green tops, diagonally into 2- to 3-inch lengths. Cut the cabbage into 3-inch pieces. Remove the stems from the mushrooms if they are tough; leave the mushrooms whole or, if very large, cut into halves. If the bamboo shoots are fresh, boil for fifteen minutes or until just tender; if tinned, drain well. Cut into ¼-inch thick slices. Drain the bean curd and cut into 1½-inch squares. Arrange the meat and vegetables attractively on large platters.

Heat the stock and taste for seasoning, correcting if necessary. Pour into a *donabe* or other large, flame-proof pot. Put the pot over a portable gas ring in the centre of the dining-table. The heat should be strong enough to keep the stock at a slow boil.

Provide each guest with a pair of chopsticks or a fondue fork, a bowl and a small saucer of the dipping sauce. Each guest dips a slice of the beef or a piece of vegetable into the broth and cooks it until it is done. It is then dipped into the sauce and eaten immediately. Do not overcook the beef or it will become hard and tasteless. Replenish the broth from time to time, keeping the level at a suitable height.

Mix the horseradish to a smooth paste with a little water. Have on the table extra soy sauce, lemon juice, and a small container of *wasabi* horseradish so that each guest can adjust his sauce to taste. When all the meat and vegetables are eaten the broth is usually drunk as a soup. Plain boiled rice is the usual accompaniment to *shabu-shabu*.

BUTANABE (Pork Casserole)

2 lb lean pork, sliced thin
½ head of Chinese cabbage
1 piece bean curd, *tōfu* (about 1lb)
½ lb chrysanthemum leaves
2 quarts water
1 10–inch piece of kelp, *kombu* seaweed
4 tablespoons *sake*

½ cup light soy sauce
4 tablespoons *mirin*
2–3 tablespoons vinegar or lemon juice
Monosodium glutamate
1–2 spring onions
1 2-inch piece fresh ginger root
1 4-inch piece *daikon* radish

This dish calls for a *kombu* stock, but if *kombu* seaweed is unavailable any type of chicken stock may be substituted. To make *kombu* stock submerge the piece of *kombu* seaweed in the cold water, add the *sake* and allow to stand for four hours. Bring the stock to the boil and remove the seaweed. Remove the stock from the fire; it is now ready to use.

The pork should be cut on a slicing machine into wafer-thin slices.

Prepare the vegetables by cutting the cabbage into 3-inch lengths and the soy bean curd into 1½-inch squares. Wash the chrysanthemum leaves and drain well. Arrange the vegetables and pork attractively on large platters.

Make a dipping sauce by mixing together the soy sauce, *mirin*, vinegar, or lemon juice and a dash of monosodium glutamate. Have on the table bowls of finely chopped green onion, including the green tops, grated ginger root and grated *daikon* radish.

Butanabe is cooked and eaten in the same way as *shabu-shabu*. A pot of the hot stock is put on a gas ring in the centre of the table, the meat and vegetables being added gradually and eaten as they become ready. Add salt as the food cooks. Each guest has his own saucer of sauce into which he dips each piece of food. Sauce should be adjusted to taste by adding the chopped onion, grated radish, or grated ginger.

CHIRINABE (*Fish and Vegetable Casserole*)

1½ lb fish (bream, cod, plaice, squid, haddock, prawns, clams, etc are suitable)
2 quarts fish or chicken stock
¼ cup *sake*
¾ lb Chinese cabbage
6 spring onions
½ lb chrysanthemum leaves

1 piece soy bean curd, *tōfu* (about 1 lb)
½ cup light soy sauce
4 tablespoons *mirin*
2–3 tablespoons lemon juice
Monosodium glutamate
2-inch piece of fresh ginger root

Clean and de-scale the fish and cut into pieces. The fish is usually chopped with the bones included, but filleted fish may be used if preferred. If prawns are used de-vein and shell, leaving only the tail shells intact. Clean and prepare the vegetables, cutting the spring onions into 3-inch lengths, the cabbage into 3-inch pieces and the drained bean curd into 1-inch squares. Arrange attractively on large platters. Add the *sake* to the stock and bring to the boil in a *donabe* or other flame-proof casserole.

Make a dipping sauce by mixing together the soy sauce, *mirin*, lemon juice and a dash of monosodium glutamate. Peel or scrape the ginger root and grate finely. Put the grated ginger into a separate bowl to be added to the sauce as desired.

Chirinabe is cooked in the same way as *shabu-shabu*. The boiling stock is put on a gas ring in the centre of the dining-table, the fish and vegetables added to the stock and eaten as soon as they are cooked. Each guest should have his own sauce bowl, to which he adds as much ginger as he fancies.

YOSENABE

½ lb boned chicken	6-inch piece fish sausage,
½ lb lean pork	*kamaboko* (optional)
¼ lb prawns	1 lb noodles (half *udon* and half
½ lb Chinese cabbage	*soba*)
3 spring onions	2 quarts chicken stock
¼ lb chrysanthemum leaves or	½ cup soy sauce
spinach	2 tablespoons *sake*
1 carrot	Monosodium glutamate
12 dried or fresh mushrooms	
1 piece bean curd, *tōfu*	
(about 1 lb)	

Yosenabe means literally 'odds and ends pot', so any or all of the above ingredients may be used, or indeed almost any meat or vegetable. Remove the chicken from the bone and cut into strips. Have the pork sliced as thin as bacon. Clean, de-vein and shell the prawns, leaving the tails intact. Cut the Chinese cabbage into pieces approximately 3 inches by 1½ inches. Drain the bean curd and cut into 1½-inch squares. Cut the spring onions diagonally into 2-inch lengths. Wash the spinach or chrysanthemum leaves carefully and remove any tough stalks. Cut the carrot into slices and parboil. If dried mushrooms are used, soak in cold water for fifteen minutes, then drain and remove hard stems; if fresh mushrooms, wash and cut away any tough part of the stems. Slice the fish sausage in ½-inch widths. If using dried noodles instead of fresh, boil until tender (*see* page 63). In Japan half *udon* noodles and half *soba* noodles are used in this dish, but if not available *lasagne* noodles may be substituted.

Prepare the cooking stock by heating together the chicken stock, soy sauce, *sake* and a dash of monosodium glutamate. When it comes to the boil, pour into a flame-proof pot and put on a portable gas ring in the centre of the dining-table. Surround the pot of stock with carefully arranged platters of the meat, fish and vegetables. Add them to the boiling stock a little at a time, serving as they become ready. Usually the strongly flavoured foods are saved till last, and the noodles are cooked last of all. Any of the dipping sauces given in the preceding recipes may be served with *yosenabe*, but its usual accompaniment is a liberal sprinkling of the Japanese pepper, *shichimi*.

YUDŌFU (*Simmered Bean Curd*)

Although unlikely to appeal to many western palates, this dish is included as being typical of the simple, delicate flavours inherent in Kyoto cooking. It is a highly nourishing dish since bean curd consists almost entirely of protein.

1 10-inch piece of kelp, *kombu* seaweed	DIPPING SAUCE
2 quarts water	1 cup light soy sauce
6 squares bean curd, *tōfu* (about 6 lb)	¼ cup *mirin*
¾ lb chrysanthemum leaves	½ oz dried *katsuobushi* flakes
12–18 fresh mushrooms (optional)	1 lemon
	1 spring onion
	1 2-inch piece of fresh ginger root

Make a *kombu* stock by immersing the piece of *kombu* seaweed in cold water and letting it stand three or four hours. Bring to the boil and discard the piece of seaweed. The stock is now ready to use. Drain the bean curd and cut into 1½-inch squares. Wash the chrysanthemum leaves and the mushrooms and drain well. Arrange the bean curd and vegetables on platters.

Make the dipping sauce by heating together the soy sauce, *mirin*, and the *katsuobushi* flakes. When it reaches the boiling point remove from the fire and strain. Pour into individual sauce bowls and put on the dining-table along with bowls of the lemon cut in sections, the spring onion finely chopped and the ginger grated finely.

Bring the *kombu* stock to the boil in a *donabe* or other flame-proof casserole and put on a gas ring in the centre of the dining-table. Keep the stock at a low boil. Add the bean curd and let it simmer gently until warmed through. Give each guest an individual bowl of the warm sauce, to which he adds lemon juice, finely chopped spring onion or grated ginger to taste. Each guest helps himself from the pot and dips the bean curd into the sauce before eating. The chrysanthemum leaves and mushrooms should be cooked last of all.

MIZUTAKI

5 lb young spring chicken
2 quarts water
Salt
1-inch piece of fresh ginger root
1 onion
¼ head of Chinese cabbage
12 large fresh mushrooms
1 piece of grilled bean curd,
    yakidōfu
½ lb bamboo shoots
12 spring onions

DIPPING SAUCE
¾ cup light soy sauce
6 tablespoons vinegar
6 tablespoons lemon juice
½ teaspoon monosodium glutamate
3 spring onions
4-inch piece daikon radish
3 finely chopped red peppers

Prepare the chicken by chopping it into 2-inch pieces with the bone and skin intact. Put the chicken, the onion quartered, the ginger sliced into five or six pieces and salt to taste in a large saucepan. Cover with the water and slowly bring to the boil, skimming away any scum which accumulates. Simmer slowly, keeping the stock clear, until the chicken is tender (about one hour).

Meanwhile wash the vegetables. Cut the cabbage into pieces about 3 inches by 1½ inches. Cut the mushrooms in half, removing any tough stems. Drain the bean curd and cut into squares. If the bamboo shoots are fresh parboil until tender; if tinned drain them well. Cut into slices ¼ inch thick. Drain the bean curd and cut into 1½-inch squares. Cut the spring onions, including green tops, into 3-inch lengths. Arrange the vegetables attractively on platters.

Make a dipping sauce by mixing the soy sauce, vinegar, lemon juice, and a dash of monosodium glutamate together. Have on the table bowls of grated daikon radish, minced green onion and minced red pepper which guests add to their own sauce to taste.

To cook and serve the mizudaki put a gas ring in the centre of the dining-table, bringing the simmering chicken and stock to it. Add a selection of the vegetables, let the mixture come to the boil again and simmer until the vegetables are tender, which will take only a few minutes. Guests help themselves to vegetables and chicken from the simmering pot, dip the pieces into their individual sauce bowls and eat immediately.

BOTAN-NABE (Wild Boar Casserole)

The boar has been hunted for centuries in Japan and its meat has always been a highly prized delicacy, especially during the winter. The Budhist taboo on eating meat was evaded by calling it *yama-kujira*, or mountain whale, a name by which it is still sometimes known. Although boar meat is unlikely to be readily obtainable in many parts of Europe, we include this most interesting recipe for the fortunate few who can come by the ingredients.

2 lb wild boar, *inoshishi*	1 quart *dashi* or other stock
1 piece bean curd, *tōfu* (about 1 lb)	½ teaspoon monosodium glutamate
6 spring onions	1 tablespoon *sake*
2 burdock roots	½ lb white bean paste, *shiro-miso*
½ lb *shirataki* noodles	1 teaspoon sugar

Have the boar meat cut in slices as thin as bacon, as for *sukiyaki*. Wrap the bean curd in a clean cloth and press firmly to remove some of its water. Cut into 1½-inch squares. Scrape the burdock roots with the back of a knife, cut into pieces about 2 inches long and drop into cold water to prevent discoloration. Wash the spring onions and cut them, green tops as well, on the bias into sections about ¼ inch wide. Drain the *shirataki* noodles. Arrange all the ingredients on large platters. Bring the stock to the boil and pour into a flame-proof casserole. Season with the monosodium glutamate and *sake*. Place the casserole on a gas ring in the centre of the dining-table and bring the stock to the boil again. Add the bean paste and the sugar. Then add a few slices of the boar meat and some of the vegetables. Gradually mix the bean paste into the stock as the meat and vegetables cook. Let guests help themselves as ingredients become ready, and continue to replenish the casserole until all the meat and vegetables are cooked. Add more stock if necessary. The liquid which remains at the end is usually drunk as a soup.

TEPPAN-YAKI STEAK

Teppan-yaki means literally 'iron-plate grilling'. This type of cooking, too, is usually done in front of guests on a large, rectangular griddle, but it can be done equally well in a large, heavy-bottomed frying pan in the privacy of the kitchen.

6 small steaks	DIPPING SAUCE
6 prawns	$\frac{3}{4}$ cup light soy sauce
3 green peppers	1 teaspoon sugar
3 spring onions	1 tablespoon *mirin*
2 cloves garlic (optional)	3 tablespoons finely chopped
10 oz fresh bean sprouts	spring onion
(optional)	2 lemons
Salt, pepper, soy sauce, *sake*	

Salt and pepper the steaks and let them stand while the other ingredients are being prepared. Clean and de-vein the prawns, removing the head and shells but leaving the tail piece intact. Slice along the inner side and open out flat. Sprinkle with a little salt and *sake*. Cut the spring onions, including tops, diagonally into 2-inch lengths. Remove the membranes, seeds and stems from the green peppers and cut lengthwise into quarters. Chop the garlic finely. Wash and drain the bean sprouts.

Make a dipping sauce by mixing together the soy sauce, sugar, *mirin* and chopped spring onion. Cut the lemons in quarters.

Heat the *teppan* or frying pan until very hot, then brush lightly with a little salad oil. Put on the steak, salt and pepper it lightly, and sauté quickly. Cook to the desired degree and remove. Add the chopped garlic, if desired, then the shrimp, green peppers, and spring onions. Season with a little soy sauce, salt and pepper and when just tender remove. Last of all sauté the bean sprouts in the same way as the other vegetables. They cook quickly and will take only two or three minutes. Serve the steak, shrimp and vegetables on warmed plates. Give each guest an individual saucer of the dipping sauce and let him season it to taste with lemon juice. Hot Chinese mustard is also a good accompaniment to this dish.

TEPPAN-YAKI DUCK

2 ducks
3 green peppers
3 leeks
1 large onion
½ lb bamboo shoots
Light soy sauce
Salt
Pepper

DIPPING SAUCE
¾ cup light soy sauce
1 teaspoon sugar
1 tablespoon *mirin*
3 tablespoons finely chopped
   spring onion
2 lemons

This is cooked in the same way as the *teppan-yaki* steak above. The duck should be cut in slices off the bone. Prepare the vegetables by cutting the green peppers into quarters, the white part of the leeks into 2-inch pieces, and the onion in ¼-inch thick slices. If fresh bamboo shoots are used boil until tender; if tinned, drain well. Slice into pieces ¼ inch thick.

Heat the *teppan* or frying pan until very hot and brush with a little salad oil. Add a few pieces of the duck, sauté quickly and keep the heat high. Add a few of the vegetables and season with salt, pepper and soy sauce. Do not try to cook everything at once, but serve the duck and vegetables as they become ready.

Give each guest an individual saucer of the dipping sauce, made by mixing together the soy sauce, sugar, *mirin*, and spring onion. Cut the lemons into quarters and allow guests to add lemon juice to taste.

DOTENABE (Oyster Casserole)

1½ lb oysters (clams, prawns, or
   other shell fish may be
   substituted)
1 piece bean curd, *tōfu* (about 1 lb)
3 spring onions
½ lb chrysanthemum leaves or
   fresh spinach

4 oz *shirataki* noodles (optional)
1 quart *dashi* or chicken stock
½ lb white bean paste, *shiro-miso*
½ teaspoon monosodium
   glutamate
2 tablespoons *sake*

Wash the oysters in cold salted water and drain. Wrap the bean curd in a clean cloth and press firmly to remove excess water. Cut the bean curd into 1½-inch squares. Wash the chrysanthemum leaves or spinach and shake off excess water. Cut the spring onions, including green tops, diagonally into ¼-inch widths. Drain the *shirataki* noodles. Arrange all the ingredients attractively on large platters. Put the soup stock into an earthenware or other heavy flame-proof casserole and bring to the boil. Season with monosodium glutamate and *sake*. Remove the casserole to a gas ring in the centre of the dining-table and let the stock come to the boil again. Put the bean paste into one side of the casserole and the oysters and a few of the vegetables into the other. Mix the bean paste gently into the soup as the vegetables and oysters cook. Let guests help themselves to the oysters and vegetables as they become ready. Replenish the casserole with stock, vegetables and oysters until all the ingredients are cooked.

GENGHIS KHAN

1½ lb lamb or beef cutlets	12 fresh mushrooms
2 tablespoons *sake*	6 spring onions
1 tablespoon soy sauce	1 small eggplant
2 tablespoons finely chopped	3 green peppers
leek	½ lb chrysanthemum leaves or
2 onions	spinach

The meat should be cut into slices ¼ inch thick. Soak in a marinade of the *sake*, soy sauce and chopped leek for two to three hours. Cut the onion into slices and the spring onions, including green tops, into 2-inch lengths. Wash the mushrooms and remove the stems. Slice the eggplant without peeling into ¼-inch thick pieces. Wash the chrysanthemum leaves or spinach carefully, removing any tough stems from the spinach. Shake off excess water. Arrange the vegetables on one platter and the meat on another.

Genghis Khan is normally cooked on a special pan over charcoal in the middle of the dining-table, but in the absence of these facilities it can be made perfectly satisfactorily in a heavy frying pan. Heat the *Genghis Khan* pan or frying pan until hot and grease with a 2-inch piece of suet. When it has melted slightly add a few pieces of the meat and vegetables, keeping the heat high. Cook until just barely done. Vegetables should remain crisp. Serve the meat and vegetables immediately as they become ready with both of the following sauces. Give each guest an individual sauce bowl, letting him help himself to the sauce of his preference.

SAUCE I

$\frac{3}{4}$ cup *sake*	$\frac{1}{2}$ to $\frac{3}{4}$ teaspoon cayenne pepper
$\frac{3}{4}$ cup grated apple	1 teaspoon grated ginger root
$\frac{3}{4}$ cup finely chopped leek	$\frac{1}{2}$ teaspoon grated garlic

Combine all the ingredients.

SAUCE II

2 tablespoons white sesame seeds	1 teaspoon sesame seed oil
1 cup *dashi* or chicken stock	$\frac{1}{2}$ teaspoon finely sliced red peppers
$\frac{1}{2}$ cup light soy sauce	1 tablespoon lemon juice or
$1\frac{1}{2}$ tablespoons dark soy sauce	vinegar

Toast the sesame seeds in a dry frying pan until they begin to jump, shaking and stirring constantly to prevent scorching. Remove from the fire and crush in a *suribachi* or mortar or put through a nut grinder. Add the soup stock, either hot or cold, stirring to prevent lumps forming. Add the other ingredients and blend well.

JAPANESE FONDUE BOURGUIGNONNE

As its name implies this dish is a variant of the Swiss fondue. It is obviously of recent origin but during the last few years has achieved great popularity in the big cities. It has almost nothing in common with traditional Japanese cooking, but does show how fashionable European dishes are adapted to the Japanese taste.

$\frac{1}{2}$ lb beef fillet	Thyme
2 green peppers	*Sake*
$\frac{1}{2}$ lb pork tenderloin	1 clove of garlic
$\frac{1}{2}$ lb firm white fish	2 spring onions
$\frac{1}{2}$ lb champignons	1 to $1\frac{1}{2}$ pints vegetable oil
$\frac{1}{2}$ lb prawns	
1 small eggplant	
Salt	BATTER
Pepper	2 eggs
Soy sauce	$\frac{2}{3}$ cup water
Mirin	1 cup cornflour
1-inch piece of fresh ginger root	$\frac{1}{2}$ teaspoon salt

Cut the meat, fish, and vegetables into cubes roughly an inch square.

The champignons should be left whole. Clean the prawns, remove shells and de-vein. Depending on their size, leave whole or cut into halves. Arrange on skewers in any combination you wish, but it is suggested that a good arrangement would be beef and green peppers, pork and eggplant, fish and mushrooms, and prawns and spring onions. Any type of skewers will do, but Japanese skewers made from bamboo are especially good since they don't transmit heat. Season the beef with salt, pepper and mashed garlic, and the pork with salt, pepper and grated ginger root. Sprinkle the fish with salt, pepper, thyme and a little *sake*. Marinate the prawns for fifteen minutes in one part soy sauce, one part *mirin* and a little grated ginger.

To make the batter blend the cornflour into the water and add the eggs, well-beaten, and the salt. Pour the batter into a deep container.

Fill a fondue pot with clean oil, and heat. Give each guest a plate covered with an absorbent square of paper. When the oil becomes hot enough, each guest selects a brochette, dips it into the batter and then into the oil until it is done. The brochette is then drained on the absorbent paper and eaten as it is or with a sprinkling of lemon juice.

FISH AND SHELLFISH

His Majesty the Emperor of Japan is a marine biologist of considerable eminence, and his interests are peculiarly appropriate to the sovereign of a people devoted, as the Japanese are, to seafood. The waters surrounding the islands of Japan abound in creatures of such variety, beauty, and palatability that not only is the eating of seafood virtually a daily habit, but Japanese folklore abounds in fishy references, and there are fish deities and fish stories galore. On the level of low humour, the fishmonger in Japan enjoys a reputation for amorous opportunity and success somewhat akin to that of the milkman in England or the iceman in America.

Even in areas far from the sea fresh-water fish are farmed, and a celebratory meal of any kind, even among the poorest people, is inconceivable without some kind of fish. We have eaten a seven course dinner consisting entirely of seafood without the least sense of monotony, and there are specialized restaurants in Japan which serve only carp, or crab, or eel, and so on.

To visit a Japanese market and contemplate the treasures of the ocean laid out for sale, fresh, glossy, and entirely free from any fishy smell is a joy to the eye and a stimulus to the palate, and although fish sold in Japan is by no means necessarily cheap, it is so good that the Japanese preference for fish over meat is easy to understand.

We do not, however, offer any recipe for *fugu* or blowfish, which is vastly popular in Japan. The flavour of the fish is pleasant enough, but not so outstanding as to justify the fuss made of it. Its popularity is due, we believe, entirely to the fact that to eat it is a little like playing Russian roulette. Unless it is prepared with the utmost care, *fugu* is highly toxic and the death of the unwary eater ensues in a matter of minutes. Although *fugu* cooks must have a special licence in Japan, the fish claims a few dramatic victims every year. Apart from *fugu*, the fish dishes of Japan are as innocuous as they are delicious, and form a whole series of jewels in the diadem of the Japanese cuisine.

TEMPURA

Tempura, probably the best-known of Japanese dishes in the West, simply consists of pieces of fish and vegetables dipped in batter and fried in deep oil. It is distinguished from the too often heavy and sodden fried foods of the West by its crisp lightness and delicacy of flavour. The superb delicacy of good *tempura* is achieved by using fresh vegetable oil and freshly-made batter, and by serving the *tempura* within seconds of its emergence from the cooking oil. In restaurants the *tempura* master does his cooking in front of his customers, placing a fresh piece of *tempura* directly on a customer's plate as he takes it from the oil. It is then dipped into a thick warm sauce called *tentsuyu*, or into plain salt, and eaten.

INGREDIENTS FOR FRYING

12 large prawns

6 fillets of white fish (smelt are particularly suitable)

1 lotus root

6 fresh mushrooms

3 green peppers

1 eggplant

1 onion

Chrysanthemum leaves

1 small bamboo shoot

1 tablespoon vinegar

Salt

Monosodium glutamate

Sake (optional)

Any or all of the above ingredients may be used, or indeed almost any other vegetable or fish. We have on occasion eaten *tempura* quail eggs, sweet potato, fresh ginger, pickled plums, seaweed, and even ice cream (which does remarkably little for either the ice cream or the *tempura*).

Shell and de-vein the prawns, leaving the tails intact. Wash and dry

the fillets of fish and cut into pieces no larger than 3 inches long and
$1\frac{1}{2}$ inches wide. Pare the lotus root and slice into $\frac{1}{4}$-inch widths. Drop
into cold, vinegared water to prevent discoloration. Wash the mush-
rooms and leave whole. Remove the stems and membranes of the green
peppers and cut into slices about 1 inch wide. Slice the onion and eggplant into $\frac{1}{4}$-inch thick rings. Wash the chrysanthemum leaves and shake
dry. Cut the bamboo shoot into $\frac{1}{4}$-inch widths. Salt all the vegetables
and sprinkle the fish and prawns with a little salt, monosodium glutamate and *sake* if available.

BATTER

1 egg	$\frac{1}{4}$ cup cornflour
$\frac{3}{4}$ cup flour	$\frac{1}{2}$ cup water

Make the batter just before using. Beat the egg and add the cold water,
beating until light. Mix the flour and cornflour and sift it into the egg
mixture. Mix lightly and quickly with a few strokes. It is most important
not to overmix. A batter containing a few lumps is perfectly satisfactory.
Experts consider a heavier batter preferable for vegetables and a thinner
one for fish, but in any case a sticky batter is not desirable, because it
produces a heavy, soggy *tempura*. If necessary thin the batter by adding
a little water gradually until it is the right consistency.

COOKING

1 to $1\frac{1}{2}$ pints vegetable oil
$\frac{1}{4}$ to $\frac{1}{2}$ cup sesame oil (optional: its addition to the vegetable oil imparts
a distinctive nutty flavour to the *tempura*)

Heat 2 to 3 inches of clean oil to a temperature of 340° to 355° F. Make
sure that the vegetables and fish are thoroughly dry. Dip each piece of
vegetable or fish into the batter, slide gently into the hot oil and cook
until light golden brown. In general, the pieces of fish and vegetable are
completely covered with batter before cooking; the exceptions are green
peppers and chrysanthemum leaves which are only half immersed,
leaving the other half uncovered. Do not put all the ingredients into the
batter at once, but dip each piece in separately just before cooking. Be
careful not to cook too many pieces at once or the temperature of the oil
will be unduly lowered. When light brown and done, remove each piece
to a rack covered with absorbent paper and drain for a second or two;
then serve immediately while still hot and crisp.

Great care must be taken to maintain the proper temperature of the oil. If too hot, the oil will burn the batter and if too cool the *tempura* will taste oily. If a thermometer is not available the temperature can be checked by dropping a little of the batter into the oil. If it submerges slightly, then rises quickly to the surface where it browns in about forty-five seconds the temperature is correct. If it remains on the surface the temperature is too high; if it sinks to the bottom and only slowly rises again the oil is too cool. Part of the secret of good *tempura* making is to keep the oil scrupulously clean by skimming away all the loose drops of batter.

TENTSUYU DIPPING SAUCE

1 cup *dashi* or chicken stock	Monosodium glutamate
⅓ cup *mirin*	1 6-inch piece of *daikon* radish or
⅓ cup light soy sauce	turnip

Mix together the broth, *mirin*, soy sauce, and monosodium glutamate. Heat to boiling point and remove from the fire, but keep warm. Grate the radish. Pour a little of the warm sauce into individual sauce bowls and put a heap of the grated radish in the centre. Each guest should mix the radish into the sauce with his chopsticks, then dip each piece of *tempura* into it before it is eaten.

HARUSAME TEMPURA

Harusame are fine noodles made from soy bean powder. When they are submerged in hot oil they puff up, making a very attractive and rather impressive coating for *tempura*.

1 lb white fish (smelt are particularly suitable)	6 green peppers
	Salt
12 prawns	Monosodium glutamate
¾ cup flour or cornflour	*Sake*
2 egg whites	1 to 1½ pints vegetable oil
2 cups cut *harusame* noodles	

The fish favoured by the Japanese for this type of *tempura* is *kisu*, a small white freshwater fish which is similar in flavour and size to smelt.

However, fillets of any white fish such as cod, plaice, hake, etc are perfectly satisfactory. Remove the head and shells of the prawns, leaving the tail shells intact. Wash carefully and de-vein. Sprinkle a little salt, monosodium glutamate and *sake* over the prawns and the fish and let stand for thirty minutes. Clean the green peppers, removing seeds, stems, and membranes and cut into quarters. Cut the *harusame* noodles with scissors into $\frac{1}{4}$- to $\frac{1}{2}$-inch lengths. Put the flour into a shallow bowl, and the egg whites into another, beating with a fork until they become light and slightly foamy but not so long that they become stiff.

Roll the fish and prawns first in the flour, then dip into the beaten egg white, then into the *harusame* noodles. Heat 2 to 3 inches of clean vegetable oil to a temperature of 340° to 355° F. When the oil is hot enough, carefully drop in two or three pieces of the coated fish and prawn. Since the noodle coating will immediately puff out, expanding considerably, do not crowd the pan by cooking too many pieces at once. Remove from the oil when the noodles are just on the point of changing colour: they should not actually brown. Drain for a moment on absorbent paper, then serve immediately while still very hot. *Harusame tempura* may be eaten either with salt or with the *tentsuyu* dipping sauce given in the recipe above.

SASHIMI (*Raw Seafood*)

There always seems to be one item in any exotic cuisine at which even the open-minded and adventurous westerner jibs. Some of these specialties, like sheep's eyeballs or fried locusts, are understandably difficult to feel peckish about, but it seems to us odd that many westerners visiting Japan, who would think nothing of downing a steak tartare or a dozen oysters on the half shell, look queasy at the thought of eating raw fish. Brave souls who do try this most inspiring and beautiful of delicacies may not always immediately experience conversion, but are unanimous in remarking in some surprise that it doesn't taste 'fishy'. It certainly does not. The coolly firm but tender flesh of really fresh fish has a generic taste which is quite indescribable, and each variety brings to the palate some subtle variant, from the virginal purity of bream to the simplicity of ordinary tuna and the slightly decadent, melting insidiousness of that part of the tuna known in Japan as *toro*. Some kinds, like octopus, squid, or abalone are chewy and resilient, others seem to dissolve on the tongue.

Even in Japan good *sashimi* is never cheap and is often ruinously expensive. This is not merely due to expense account snobbery, but reflects the fact that only the best part of the freshest of prime fish will do. If the western cook bears this in mind, his or her guests may try this delicacy in full confidence that there will be no upset stomachs to mar the morning after.

1 lb raw seafood (sea-bream, tuna, sole, smelt, cuttlefish, turbot, halibut, abalone, trout, etc)	2 tablespoons Japanese horseradish, *wasabi*
½ lb Japanese radish, *daikon*	½ cup light soy sauce
1 bunch watercress or other garnish	

As we noted above, only the freshest fish of the highest quality should be used for *sashimi*, and in fact, in Japanese restaurants the fish are often kept alive in tubs until the moment of preparation. Almost any fish is suitable for *sashimi* and the ones listed above are simply those most commonly used in Japan. Either a mixture of seafood or a single kind of fish may be used. The dark red of tuna and the white of sea-bream make it one of the most favoured combinations in Japan.

Clean the fish carefully, removing all bones and skin. Put the resulting fish fillets into a colander, pour boiling water over them and immediately immerse in cold water. (The object of this exercise is not to cook the fish in any way, but simply to give some protection against surface bacteria.) There are various ways of cutting the flesh of the fish. It is usually sliced into pieces 1½ inches long, 1 inch wide, and ¼ inch thick, but it can also be cut into cubes or wafers, a shape favoured for small, delicate fish such as smelt or trout. Grate the radish on a grater with large holes. *Sashimi* is always served in individual bowls and great care is taken that the colour and shape of the container enhances the appearance of the fish. Put a mound of two or three tablespoons of the grated radish into each bowl and on one side of the mound arrange attractively six to eight slices of the fish. Garnish with a sprig of watercress, other greenery, or a tiny flower. In Japan various garnishes are used, sometimes edible, sometimes not, the most common being the leaves of *kinome*, a highly scented pepper plant; a sprig of *shiso*, or perilla; the yellow buds of the rape plant; or tiny, whole, flowering cucumbers.

Obviously there is great scope for imagination here, and the ordinary back garden should yield several attractive garnishes.

Mix the horseradish with a little water into a paste of mustard-like consistency and put a teaspoonful in each bowl beside the fish. Give each guest a separate, shallow sauce bowl containing two tablespoons light soy sauce. Each guest mixes as much of the horseradish as he desires into his soy sauce, then picks up a piece of fish with chopsticks and dips it into the sauce before eating it.

Variations of the basic soy sauce which are occasionally used are as follows:

I $\frac{1}{2}$ cup soy sauce, 1 tablespoon grated ginger root
II $\frac{1}{2}$ cup soy sauce, 1 tablespoon hot mustard
III $\frac{1}{2}$ cup soy sauce, 2 tablespoons lemon juice
IV $\frac{1}{2}$ cup soy sauce, 2 tablespoons dried bonito flakes, simmered and strained.

TAI SHIO-YAKI (Sea-bream Grilled with Salt)

Of all the ways of grilling fish in Japan that of *shio-yaki*, or 'salt-roast', is undoubtedly the best for bringing out the true flavour of the fish rather than concealing it. Perhaps for this reason whole grilled fish in salt are the accompaniment to every festive occasion in Japan, from birthdays to christenings, marriages and engagements. The *tai* or sea-bream is thought to be especially delicious and auspicious, and there is a whole body of superstition and folklore connected with this fish. On ceremonial occasions it is always served whole, a headless fish being thought unlucky, and is invariably served with its head to the left and its belly towards the eater. In fact, from the time the fish is caught when the fisherman puts it lovingly in a basket with its head to the left and its belly to the front, this position is maintained by all handlers until the moment when the fish is placed, ready to eat, on the dining-table. This practice may lend some justification to the common belief that the upper side or 'front' of a fish tastes better than the under side.

2 fresh sea-bream   4 thin metal skewers
Salt

Carefully wash the fish and scale them. Work from the tail to the head,

taking care not to damage the skin. Turn the fish over to its under or
back side (remembering that the so-called 'front' of the fish is the side
with the head to the left and the belly facing you); make an incision just
below the pectoral fin and remove the entrails. Carefully wash out the
cavity. Sprinkle the entire fish liberally with salt. An amount weighing
1 to 2 per cent of the weight of the fish is about right. Let the fish stand
for thirty minutes by which time the salt will have dissolved. Wipe off
the moisture with a dry cloth.

Great care is taken to retain the natural shape of the fish during its
cooking and the skewers are inserted for this purpose. Oil the thin
skewers. Turn the fish over to its back side. Insert the first skewer just
below the eye and pass it through the bones and out by the tail, curving
up the tail of the fish slightly. Insert the second skewer just below the
first one and bring it out just below the tail. Be careful that the skewers
do not pierce the front side of the fish.

Cooking sea-bream over charcoal gives them far more flavour than
when a gas or electric grill is used, but if charcoal is not available heat
the grill before putting in the fish. Just before cooking sprinkle the sea-
bream with the finishing salt. Salt liberally, and in particular rub plenty
of salt into the tail and fins. This not only prevents them from burning
but also results in a light, powdery finish which greatly enhances the
appearance of the cooked fish. When the grill is hot put the fish under
it, if possible resting the skewers on the edge of a baking tin so that the
fish cooks without touching a surface. Grill the front of the fish first, for
about four minutes. Then turn it over and grill the under side for about
four minutes. Remove the fish when done and carefully take out the
skewers. Arrange the fish carefully on a plate and serve garnished with
lemon or young, tender stems of ginger.

SAKANA SHIO-YAKI (Fish Grilled with Salt)

6 small fish such as horse-mackerel   Salt
   or smelt or 6 pieces of any white
   fish

Substitute any whole white fish or fish pieces for the sea-bream and
proceed as in the above recipe.

AYU SHIO-YAKI (*Trout Grilled in Salt*)

6–12 fresh trout   ¼ cup *dashi*
Salt   Monosodium glutamate
½ cup vinegar

Japanese trout are about half the size of the European or American
variety, and so two should be allowed for one serving. Prepare the trout
in the same way as the sea-bream. Insert a single skewer into each fish,
pushing it through the mouth and out through the body as in the illus-
tration. Grill in the same way as the sea-bream. Serve with individual

saucers of *tadesu* dipping sauce, a mixture of two parts vinegar and one
part *dashi* broth. Japanese vinegar, distilled from rice, has a light,
fragrant quality which adds a good deal to this sauce, but if it is not
available use a distilled cider vinegar and one teaspoon sugar.

FISH TERIYAKI

Teriyaki refers to the cooking process of marinating foods in a sauce of
soy sauce, *mirin*, and *sake* and then grilling them, preferably over charcoal. Slightly oily fish such as mackerel, yellowfish, tuna, and so forth
are preferable to a delicately flavoured white fish for this dish. It is also
a favourite way of cooking both cuttlefish and eel.

6 pieces of fresh fish (mackerel,   6 tablespoons *mirin*
    yellowfish, etc)   6 tablespoons *sake*
6 tablespoons dark soy sauce   1 clove garlic (optional)

Mix the soy sauce, *mirin*, and *sake* together in a small saucepan and bring
to the boil. If you choose to use the garlic chop finely and add. Marinate
the fish fillets in this mixture for fifteen or twenty minutes. Preheat the
grill, and cook the fish under a moderate flame for five or ten minutes on
each side, brushing three or four times with the marinade. When done
the fish should be coated with a rich brown glaze. Serve immediately.

GRILLED FISH WITH YOLK GLAZE

This glaze made from egg yolk adds a delicate golden gloss to grilled fish and one which is, of course, far more delicately flavoured than the *teriyaki* sauce described above.

6 fillets of white fish (sea-bream, flounder, plaice, etc)	¼ teaspoon salt
1½ teaspoons salt	1 teaspoon *mirin*
1 egg yolk	Monosodium glutamate

Wipe the fish over with a damp cloth. Salt rather heavily and leave for thirty minutes. Wipe off the dissolved salt with a dry cloth. Mix together the egg yolk, salt, *mirin*, and a dash of monosodium glutamate. Preheat the grill. Brush the fish with the egg yolk mixture and grill under a medium flame for five or ten minutes on each side. Brush with the egg yolk mixture two or three times during the cooking. Remove when the fish is done and the glaze is dry. Serve immediately.

HŌRAKU-YAKI (*Fish Baked with Pine Needles*)

This is a beautiful dish. Its aroma of pine needles and its delicate hues of pink and dark green make it a fitting dish for the most formal occasion. If used for a first course these amounts should be reduced.

3 very fresh white fish (small sea-bream are used most frequently in Japan)	6 chestnuts
	Pine needles
6–12 large prawns	Salt
12 fresh mushrooms	1 lemon

Select an earthenware or oven-proof glass baking dish and cover the bottom with small, clean pebbles. Over these lay a thin bed of pine needles.

Carefully wash the fish, then scale it, taking care not to damage the skin. Do not remove the head or tail. Remove the entrails by making an incision below the pectoral fin on one side of the fish only, so that the other side will remain undamaged. Carefully wash the cavity. Sprinkle the fish heavily with salt and let stand for thirty minutes. Wipe away the moisture with a damp cloth. Make three or four diagonal cuts on the back side of each fish, that is, on the side from which the entrails were removed.

Remove the heads of the prawns. Leave the shells and tails intact, but cut along the back of the shell in order to de-vein. Wash the mushrooms, cutting away any tough stems. Use either fresh or tinned chestnuts. Arrange the fish, top side up, the prawns, chestnuts, and mushrooms on the bed of pine needles and salt liberally. Cover the dish with aluminium foil. Bake in a hot oven (400° F or Mark 7) for twenty minutes or until the fish is done. The juices from the fish and vegetables drain through the pebbles to the bottom of the pan so that they do not become soggy. If the pine needles turn brown while cooking replace with fresh ones before serving. Serve with wedges of lemon.

SAKANA UNIYAKI (Fish Grilled with Sea Chestnut Sauce)

6 fish fillets or pieces (sole, turbot, bream, plaice, flounder, etc)
2 egg yolks

2 tablespoons sea chestnut sauce, *uni*
Salt

Clean the fish carefully and salt liberally. Allow to stand for thirty minutes. Wipe the fish carefully with a dry cloth. Grill on both sides under a medium flame until the fish is half done. Remove and brush liberally with the egg yolk and sea chestnut mixture. Return to the grill and cook until done, brushing the fish two or three times with the glaze. When golden brown remove and serve immediately.

NAMAZAKE-NO-GINSHIYAKI (Salmon Baked in Foil)

6 salmon steaks
1 onion
6 thin slices of lemon

Salt
Pepper
3 tablespoons *sake*

Oil six squares of foil paper and put a salmon steak in the centre of each. Season with salt, pepper and sprinkle half a tablespoon of *sake* over each piece. Slice the onion, separate the rings, and lay four or five rings on each steak. Top with a slice of lemon. Fold the foil paper over, sealing tightly. Bake for twenty minutes in a moderate oven. Serve in the paper.

KANI-NO-GINSHIYAKI (*Crab Baked in Foil*)

1 lb crab, cooked and separated	3 tablespoons *sake*
from the shell	Salt
6 large fresh mushrooms	Pepper
6 small eggplants or one large	
eggplant	

Oil six squares of foil paper. Wash the mushrooms and leave whole. Wash the eggplants and cut in halves without peeling, scoring the skin lightly with a knife in a checkerboard pattern. The eggplants which are used for this dish in Japan are about the size of a large egg; if you use a large European eggplant cut into twelve pieces. Put one-sixth of the crab, a mushroom and two pieces of eggplant onto each piece of foil. Sprinkle with salt, pepper, monosodium glutamate and a little of the *sake*. Seal carefully and bake in a moderate oven for twenty minutes. Serve in the foil paper.

SAKANA-NO-GINSHIYAKI (*Fish Baked in Foil*)

6 fillets of white fish (cod, plaice,	1 lemon
sole, or flounder)	Salt
6 large mushrooms	Pepper
12 gingko nuts, *ginnan* or pine nuts	Monosodium glutamate

Cut six squares of foil paper and wipe one side of each with a little oil. Place a piece of fish in the centre of each piece and arrange on its top a whole mushroom, two gingko nuts and a thin slice of lemon. Season with salt, pepper, and monosodium glutamate, and if available, about half a tablespoon of *sake*. Seal the aluminium foil and bake in a medium oven (Mark 5) for fifteen to twenty minutes. Serve in the paper.

MASU-NO-GINSHIYAKI (*Trout Baked in Foil*)

6 fresh trout	Salt
1 lemon	Pepper
3 tablespoons *sake*	Monosodium glutamate

Cut six squares of aluminium foil and oil one side of each. Clean the
trout thoroughly and score the skin on one side three or four times.
Sprinkle liberally with salt. Season with a little pepper and monosodium
glutamate. Sprinkle about one-half a tablespoon of *sake* on each trout.
Let stand for ten or fifteen minutes. Put each fish on a piece of foil, top
with a thin slice of lemon and seal tightly. Bake in a medium oven
(Mark 5) for fifteen to twenty minutes. Serve in the foil.

SAKANA MISO-YAKI (Fish Cooked with Bean Paste)

Oily fish of a dense texture are preferable for this dish.

6 pieces of mackerel, bonito, tuna, etc	4 tablespoons bean paste, *miso*
½ cup *sake*	1 tablespoon sugar
¾ cup water	1 tablespoon soy sauce
	1-inch piece of fresh ginger root

Put the water, *sake*, and sugar into a wide-bottomed saucepan and bring
to the boil. Place the fish in the pan, cover with a lid and simmer until
the fish is done. Carefully remove the fish, arrange on a platter or on
individual plates and keep warm. Add the bean paste to the liquid in the
saucepan, mix and heat until it dissolves. Add the soy sauce and remove
from the heat. Pour the sauce over the fish and serve, with a sprinkling
of grated ginger on top.

GRILLED TUNA TSUKEYAKI

6 tuna steaks	2 tablespoons *mirin*
3 tablespoons dark soy sauce	½-inch piece of fresh ginger root
1 tablespoon *sake*	1 clove of garlic

Grate the ginger root and clove of garlic and mix together with the soy
sauce, *sake* and *mirin*. Wipe the tuna steaks with a damp cloth and let
them stand in the marinade fifteen minutes, turning them over once.
Heat the grill and when it becomes hot put the tuna in, grilling for about
five minutes on each side. Just before removing brush the tuna with the
marinade once more and remove as soon as the sauce has dried into a
high glaze. Serve immediately.

4

GRILLED MACKEREL TSUKEYAKI

6 mackerel steaks

Substitute mackerel for tuna and proceed as in the recipe on page 97.

SAKANA MISOZUKE (*Fish Fillets Cured in Bean Paste*)

Though it sounds unpromising this method of curing fish is extremely good, the *miso* imparting a certain richness of flavour to the fish which makes them almost as good served cold as hot.

6 fillets of fish (mackerel, bream, cod, etc)	⅓ cup *mirin*
1 lb white bean paste, *shiromiso*	2 tablespoons *sake*

Mix together the bean paste, *mirin*, and *sake*. Spread a layer of the bean paste mixture in the bottom of a flat-bottomed bowl or baking tin. Arrange the fish fillets on top and cover with the remaining bean paste. Let the fish stand in this mixture for at least six hours and preferably for twenty-four. They can, in fact, be kept in the refrigerator in the bean paste mixture for four or five days, but are best cured for one or two days. When ready to cook remove the fillets from the bean paste, carefully wipe off any vestiges of bean paste which still cling to the surface and grill on both sides until done. Serve either hot or cold.

AJI-NO-NITSUKE (*Sprats or Herrings Simmered in Soy Sauce*)

6 herrings or 12 sprats	4 tablespoons *sake*
1½ cups water	1 2-inch piece of fresh ginger root
1 tablespoon sugar	30 snow peas
½ cup soy sauce	Salt

Clean and wash the fish, removing the entrails and scales but leaving on the head and tail. On the front side of the fish cut three diagonal slits through the skin and into the flesh. Clean the ginger and cut into match-like sticks. Put the water, sugar, and soy sauce into a large-bottomed saucepan. Bring to the boil. Carefully arrange the fish on the bottom of the saucepan. If the pan will not accommodate all the fish cook them in two batches. Sprinkle the ginger over the top. Cover with a lid. In Japan a wooden lid, smaller than the saucepan, is put directly on top of the fish which has the effect of keeping them pushed down and thus helps to retain their shape. Bring the liquid to the boil again, turn down the fire to a medium flame and cook for five minutes. Turn the fire down very low and continue to simmer for fifteen minutes. Remove the saucepan from the fire and let the fish stand in the liquid for five or ten minutes before serving.

Clean the snow peas and string them. Drop into boiling, salted water and cook for two or three minutes or until they are tender. Drain. Arrange the fish on a serving dish and garnish with the snow peas.

SALMON CROQUETTES

8 oz tinned salmon	$\frac{1}{2}$-inch piece of fresh ginger
$\frac{3}{4}$ lb potatoes	2 dried mushrooms
$\frac{1}{3}$ cup hot milk	1 egg
Salt	1 teaspoon salt
Pepper	$\frac{1}{4}$ teaspoon pepper
1 small carrot	Monosodium glutamate
	$\frac{1}{2}$ cup cornflour
SAUCE SANBAIZU	1 pint vegetable oil
$\frac{1}{3}$ cup light soy sauce	1 tablespoon sugar
$\frac{1}{3}$ cup vinegar	Monosodium glutamate

Peel the potatoes, boil until tender and mash with the hot milk, salt, and pepper while still hot. Mix together with the salmon. Boil the carrot in a little salted water until tender, and chop finely. Soften the dried mushrooms in cold water, drain and mince. Peel the ginger and mince. Add the finely-chopped carrot, mushroom, and ginger to the salmon and potato mixture along with the egg, salt, pepper and monosodium glutamate. When well mixed form into balls about 1 inch in diameter. Roll the balls in the cornflour. Heat about 3 inches of oil in a pan and when hot fry a few balls at a time, cooking until well-browned. Drain for a moment on absorbent paper and serve immediately, with individual bowls of *sanbaizu* dipping sauce, made by combining the soy sauce, vinegar, sugar, and monosodium glutamate.

SABA-NO-NITSUKE (*Mackerel Simmered in Soy Sauce*)

Any type of dark, rather oily fish such as tuna is also suitable for this dish.

6 pieces of mackerel	3 tablespoons *sake*
2 cups water	½ cup soy sauce
1 tablespoon sugar	1 2-inch piece of fresh ginger root
2 tablespoons *mirin*	

Wipe the pieces of fish with a damp cloth. Cut the ginger root into paper thin slices. Put all the other ingredients into a wide-bottomed saucepan and bring to the boil. Add the mackerel and sprinkle the ginger over the top. Put a lid on the saucepan and bring the liquid to a boil again. Reduce the heat to medium and cook for five minutes. Turn the fire down very low and continue to simmer for fifteen minutes. Remove the saucepan from the fire and let the fish stand in the liquid for fifteen minutes. If necessary, re-heat before serving. Arrange the fish on a platter and serve.

KABAYAKI (*Grilled Eel*)

The Japanese have never felt the prejudice against eels which is found among so many Europeans. Indeed, eel-eating is such a popular pastime during August, when it is thought that its health-giving properties are particularly effective against the debility caused by summer heat, that eel restaurants have a difficult time keeping up with the demand. Records of this particular recipe have been found as early as the thirteenth century and its method of grilling in a reduced marinade of soy sauce and *mirin* produces a rich, succulent dish which should quell the reservations of even the most squeamish.

1 eel	½ cup *mirin*
5 tablespoons dark soy sauce	

Remove the intestines and the central backbone from the eel and cut off the head. Slice along one side and open up flat. Cut into four pieces, making four fillets. Combine in a small saucepan the soy sauce and *mirin*. Bring the mixture to the boil and reduce to about two-thirds its original volume.

Heat the grill. When hot put the eel under the grill, slightly oiling both the eel and the rack to avoid sticking. Grill each side for about five minutes. Remove and brush with the soy sauce and *mirin* mixture and return to the grill. Baste with the mixture two or three times on each side and cook for a total of about ten minutes longer, or until the eel is done and the sauce has formed a shiny glaze on its surface. Serve immediately, with a tablespoon or two of the leftover marinade poured over the top. Serves four.

SAKANA KARAAGE (*Fish Coated with Cornflour*)

In this simplest method of deep-fat frying, the fish is simply dusted with a protective coating of cornflour and immersed in the hot oil.

12 sprats or large pilchards
Salt
Cornflour
1 pint vegetable oil

1 cup *dashi*
4 tablespoons soy sauce
2 tablespoons *mirin*

Remove the head, entrails, and fins and clean the fish thoroughly. Sprinkle liberally with salt and leave for fifteen or twenty minutes. Wipe dry with a clean cloth. Bring 2 inches of vegetable oil to the right temperature for frying. Lightly dust the fish with cornflour and fry until done in the hot oil. Drain for a second on absorbent paper and serve with an accompanying saucer of sauce made from the *dashi*, soy sauce, and *mirin*, mixed together and brought to the boil.

SABA NO KARAAGE NO SUZUKE (*Fried Mackerel Simmered with Radish*)

6 pieces of mackerel
Salt
Cornflour
1 pint vegetable oil
1 cup *dashi*

1½ tablespoons *mirin*
3 tablespoons dark soy sauce
½ lb Japanese radish, *daikon*
1 spring onion

Clean the fish thoroughly and wipe dry. Salt and allow to stand for thirty

minutes. Wipe away the dissolved salt with a dry cloth. Lightly dust the
fish with cornflour. Heat the oil and when hot put in the fish and fry
until crisp. Peel and grate the radish. Cut the spring onion, including
green top, into narrow slices. Mix together the *dashi* broth, *mirin* and
soy sauce in a wide-bottomed saucepan and bring to the boil. Add the
fish and simmer for ten minutes. Add the grated radish and chopped
spring onion, bring to the boil and remove from the fire. Place the fish
in shallow bowls, pour the sauce over the top and serve immediately.

SABA NO SUTATAKI (Vinegared Mackerel)

1 mackerel	½ cup vinegar
Salt	2 tablespoons sugar
3 oz Japanese radish, *daikon*	¼ teaspoon monosodium glutamate
1 spring onion	1 lemon
3 oz carrot	Parsley
2-inch piece of fresh ginger root	

Clean the mackerel and remove the bones and skin, cutting the flesh into
slices about ¼ inch thick. Salt liberally and let stand for three or four
hours. Mix together the vinegar, sugar, and monosodium glutamate and
pour over the fish, letting it marinate in the mixture for thirty minutes.
The fish will become firm and the flesh whiten. Cut the *daikon* radish,
carrot and ginger into julienne strips. Cut the spring onion diagonally
into narrow strips about ⅛ inch wide. Remove the mackerel from the
marinade and arrange attractively on a platter. Surround the fish with
the strips of vegetables, pour the vinegar dressing over the top and allow
to marinate for ten minutes before serving. Garnish with slices of lemon
and small bunches of parsley.

IKA NO MIRINYAKI (Grilled Squid)

The squid or cuttlefish has been both neglected and despised in northern
Europe, although not along the Mediterranean coast. In Japan it is properly appreciated and its pearly whiteness and unique texture assure the
squid its place in a myriad of dishes. It is one of the most common fishes
used in *sushi* and is an addition to many salads, as well as being grilled

and stewed in a variety of fashions, probably the most popular of which is the method described below.

1 squid	¼ cup *mirin*
½ cup dark soy sauce	¼ cup *sake*

Clean the squid by removing the entrails which are enclosed in the pockets of the fish, pull out the spinal column and remove the outer skin by washing in running water. It should rub off easily. Take out the ink bags on either side of the head, then the eyes. Rinse well in running water. Cut into large squares and poach in lightly boiling salted water until the squid turns a pure, milky white. This will take no longer than five minutes. Mix together in a small saucepan the soy sauce, *mirin*, and *sake* and bring to the boil. Remove from the fire and marinate the squid in this sauce for ten minutes. Drain. Score the surface of the fish in a checkerboard pattern. Heat the grill, and when hot put the squid under it, cooking for about five minutes on each side, brushing two or three times with the sauce during the cooking. Serve immediately.

SWEET AND SOUR PRAWNS

12 prawns	1½ teaspoons sugar
1-inch piece of fresh ginger root	2½ tablespoons light soy sauce
1 teaspoon white sesame seeds	½ teaspoon salt
2 tablespoons vinegar	Monosodium glutamate

Wash the prawns. Insert toothpicks along the back ridges of the prawns in between the shell and the flesh. These will keep the prawns straight as they cook. Bring salted water to boil in a medium-sized saucepan, add the prawns and simmer for two to three minutes, until they change colour. Drain, cool slightly, and remove shells.

Put the vinegar, sugar, salt, and monosodium glutamate together in a small saucepan and heat until the sugar dissolves. Remove from the fire and pour over the prawns, letting them marinate in this mixture for one or two hours. Peel the ginger and chop finely. Add the soy sauce and cook over a low fire until the liquid has almost evaporated. Heat the sesame seeds in a dry frying pan until they begin to jump, stirring constantly to prevent burning. Arrange the marinated prawns on a plate, spread the chopped ginger over them and sprinkle the sesame seeds on top.

BOILED PRAWNS

12 large prawns   ½ teaspoon salt
1½ cups water   1 teaspoon soy sauce
2 tablespoons *mirin*

Clean the prawns, removing the heads and shells but leaving the tails
intact. Combine the water, *mirin*, salt, and soy sauce in a saucepan.
Bring to the boil. Add the prawns and cook until they turn pink. Remove,
drain and serve cold.

GRILLED PRAWNS WITH SESAME SEEDS

12 prawns   Monosodium glutamate
1 teaspoon black sesame seeds   1 lemon
2 tablespoons *sake*   Light soy sauce
Salt

Wash the prawns well and remove head and legs, but leave shells and
tails intact. Split the prawns lengthwise through the shell and open up
flat, but do not completely separate. Sprinkle the prawns with a little
salt, monosodium glutamate and *sake* and allow them to stand for fifteen
minutes. Sprinkle on the sesame seeds, and put the prawns, flesh side
up, under a hot grill for four or five minutes. Remove, then turn them
over and grill the shell side for three or four minutes. Serve on individual
plates with a sauce of equal parts of soy sauce and lemon juice.

EBI ONIGARA

12 large prawns   4 tablespoons soy sauce
4 tablespoons *mirin*   *Sansho* or *shichimi* pepper

Cut off the heads and trim away the legs of the prawns, but leave the
shells and tails intact. Cut through the underside of the prawn and open
up, spreading it out flat. Mix the *mirin* and the soy sauce together. Heat
the grill and when hot put the prawns, shell side up, under it for three
minutes. Remove and turn the prawns over, flesh side up, and brush
with the soy sauce and *mirin* mixture. Grill again until the prawns are
done and the sauce is dry and has formed a glaze. Sprinkle with *sansho*
or *shichimi* pepper if available.

MEAT AND POULTRY

In the early years of the Meiji Restoration in Japan, about a hundred years ago, western ways were adopted and recommended by leaders of opinion with a fervour that strikes modern observers as verging on the hilarious. Pundits and savants of the time urged the wholesale abandonment of Japanese ways in favour of what was thought to be the European mode. It was seriously canvassed by quite reputable persons that the Japanese language should be abolished in favour of English, that Japanese men should be permitted to marry only European women in order to improve the stock (though Japanese women were not to be permitted the same exogamous luxury, which seems very hard on them), and that the practice of Buddhism should be prohibited. An attempt was actually made to carry out the last of these suggestions, but with very limited and temporary success.

Other less alarmingly extreme suggestions debated in the new National Diet included the national diet, and the possibility of changing it so as to induce in the Japanese people the inventive and energetic habits of westerners, which were thought to be due in part to their hearty consumption of meat and dairy products. This was not so silly as it might sound, and Japanese dieticians to this day point out the deficiency in protein and fats of the food consumed by many Japanese.

Imaginative cooks soon created many dishes, such as the renowned *sukiyaki*, adapting meat to the Japanese taste, and although the modern

Japanese cuisine is still not overly rich in meat dishes, it nevertheless contains many pleasing examples, some of which we describe below.

CHICKEN TERIYAKI

1 chicken, cut into pieces
½ cup soy sauce
¼ cup *mirin*
¼ cup *sake*
1 teaspoon sugar
¼ teaspoon cayenne pepper
1 clove of garlic
1-inch piece of fresh ginger root
   (optional)
2 tablespoons oil

Mix together in a small saucepan the soy sauce, *mirin*, *sake*, sugar, red pepper and chopped garlic clove and bring to the boil. Remove at once and pour over the chicken pieces, letting them marinate in this sauce for thirty minutes, turning occasionally. Drain and dry the chicken. Heat the oil in a frying pan, add the chicken and brown. Reduce the heat and add a little of the marinade and a little water. Cover and simmer until the chicken is tender, about twenty minutes.

Teriyaki chicken may also be baked in the oven. Arrange the drained chicken pieces in a baking tin and cook uncovered in a Mark 4 oven for forty to fifty minutes. Turn the pieces after the first half hour, and baste four or five times during the cooking with the remaining marinade.

YAKITORI (*Chicken on Skewers*)

These delicious little tidbits utilize the same sauce as in the recipe above. They are hardly substantial enough for a full meal, but are an excellent accompaniment to drinks.

1 lb raw boned chicken
1 onion
4 leeks
¼ cup *sake*
2 teaspoons sugar
1 clove of garlic
2 green peppers
6 chicken livers
½ cup soy sauce
¼ cup *mirin*
1-inch piece of fresh ginger root
   (optional)
¼ teaspoon monosodium glutamate
¼ teaspoon red pepper

Cut the boned chicken into bite-size pieces. Cut the chicken livers in halves or quarters. Clean the leeks and cut into 1-inch lengths, using the white part only. Cut both the green peppers and the onion into bite-size pieces. Arrange two of the chicken pieces and one each of the pieces of green pepper, leek, onion and liver on metal or bamboo skewers, starting and ending with the chicken. If you oil the skewers they will be easier to remove later.

Chop the garlic and ginger finely and put into a small saucepan with the soy sauce, *mirin*, *sake*, sugar, monosodium glutamate and red pepper. Bring to the boil and pour over the skewered chicken, allowing it to marinate thirty minutes. Heat the grill and when hot place the kebabs under it, cooking two or three minutes on each side. Remove the kebabs, dip them into the marinade again and grill again until the chicken is done. This dish is better, of course, cooked over charcoal, but a gas or electric grill can be used with good results.

TORINIKU NO NANBANYAKI (*Grilled Chicken, Kyushu Style*)

1 chicken	3 tablespoons *sake*
3 spring onions	1½ tablespoons *mirin*
2 red peppers or ¼ teaspoon	1 tablespoon flour
cayenne pepper	¼ teaspoon monosodium glutamate
1 egg yolk	¼ cup soy sauce

Cut the chicken into pieces suitable for grilling. Mix together the *sake*, *mirin* and soy sauce and marinate the chicken in this mixture for fifteen minutes. Remove the chicken from the marinade and reserve. Chop the spring onions and red peppers very finely and add to the leftover marinade along with the egg yolk, flour and monosodium glutamate. Beat the mixture until very smooth. Grill the chicken under a medium flame for about ten minutes on each side. When the chicken is partially cooked remove and brush with the sauce. Continue cooking until done, about thirty minutes in all, brushing three or four times on each side with the sauce. The addition of the egg yolk in the sauce will produce a very high glaze, but care must be taken not to cook the chicken under too hot a grill since the sauce burns easily.

TORINIKU TATSUTA-AGE (Deep Fried Marinated Chicken)

1 chicken	1-inch piece of fresh ginger root
3 tablespoons light soy sauce	(optional)
3 tablespoons *mirin*	½ cup cornflour
¼ teaspoon red pepper	1 pint or more of vegetable oil

Cut the chicken into pieces suitable for frying. If using ginger root chop finely and put it in a small saucepan together with the soy sauce, *mirin* and red pepper. When it comes to the boil remove and pour over the chicken, letting it marinate in this mixture for thirty minutes.

Heat about 3 inches of clean vegetable oil in a deep pan. Drain the chicken, dry with a cloth and roll in the cornflour. When the oil reaches a temperature of about 350° F add the chicken, a few pieces at a time. Fry until done. Be careful not to let the oil get too hot; soy sauce burns easily and has a rather disagreeable taste when it does. When the chicken is done remove from the oil, drain for a few moments on absorbent paper and serve immediately.

TORINIKU NO SHICHIMI-YAKI (Chicken Baked in Foil)

1 chicken	1 lemon
3 spring onions	½ teaspoon *shichimi* pepper
2 tablespoons white sesame seeds	¼ teaspoon monosodium glutamate
½ cup light soy sauce	1 tablespoon oil
2 teaspoons sugar	Foil paper

Cut the chicken into large neat pieces. Toast the sesame seeds in a dry frying pan until they begin to jump. Remove and crush in a *suribachi* or mortar, or by putting them through a nut grinder. Mince the onions. Mix both the crushed sesame seeds and the onions together with the soy sauce, sugar and monosodium glutamate and marinate the chicken in this sauce for thirty minutes. Cut a piece of foil paper for each piece of chicken, large enough to enclose it securely. Oil each piece. Place a piece of chicken in the centre of each piece of paper, sprinkle with a little *shichimi* pepper, put a slice of lemon on top and wrap well. Bake in a medium oven for thirty minutes or until the chicken is done.

TORINIKU TO SHIITAKE NO TERIYAKI
(*Sautéed Chicken and Mushrooms*)

These cocktail tidbits, attractive though they are, are rather tedious to make. For an ordinary family dinner the mushrooms and chicken may simply be cut in cubes and cooked in the same way as the brochettes.

1 lb chicken breasts	2 tablespoons *mirin*
10–12 large fresh mushrooms	2 teaspoons sugar
2 tablespoons oil	¼ teaspoon monosodium glutamate
4 tablespoons soy sauce	

Bone and skin the chicken breasts and cut the meat into very thin slices. Wash the mushrooms and remove the stems. Cut the mushrooms into ¾-inch cubes. Roll a slice of chicken around the mushrooms and arrange several of these rolls on a bamboo skewer. Heat the oil in a frying pan and add the brochettes, sautéeing quickly until the chicken browns. Remove the oil from the pan and add the soy sauce, *mirin*, sugar and monosodium glutamate, sautéeing for three or four minutes longer and shaking the frying pan back and forth to ensure that the brochettes are well covered with the sauce. Remove and serve, hot or cold.

DRUNK CHICKEN ASHIYA

This delicious dish is a speciality of the Ashiya Steak House in Kyoto, where it is served as an appetizer.

1 lb boned chicken	2 green peppers
¾ cup *sake*	1 onion
1½ tablespoons soy sauce	2 tablespoons oil
¼ teaspoon monosodium glutamate	1–2 teaspoons soy sauce

The chicken should be young and tender. Cut it into cubes about ¾ inch square and marinate in the *sake* and soy sauce for eight hours. Take out the seeds and membranes from the green peppers and cut both the green peppers and the onion into ½-inch squares. Heat the oil in a frying pan and cook the onions and green peppers until tender. Do not brown. Drain the chicken and add to the frying pan, sautéeing quickly. It should be cooked the minimum time possible. Add one to two teaspoons soy sauce, remove from the fire and serve immediately.

TORINIKU NO AWAYUKI-AGE (*Chicken Tempura*)

1 lb chicken breasts	3 tablespoons cold water
2–3 tablespoons flour	⅓ cup flour
Salt	1 egg white
Pepper	1 pint or more of vegetable oil
1 egg yolk	

Bone and skin the chicken breasts, cutting the meat into pieces about 2–3 inches long and ¾ inch in diameter. Bring a shallow saucepan of water to the boil and dip each piece of chicken into the boiling water, leaving until it slightly firms. Remove and drain well. Sprinkle lightly with salt and pepper, and roll in a little flour. Make a batter by separating the egg and mixing the yolk with the water. Add ⅓ cup flour and mix quickly and lightly, not worrying too much about lumps. Beat the egg white until it is stiff and fold it lightly into the batter.

Heat about three inches of oil to a suitable temperature for frying (355° F). Dip the chicken pieces into the batter and fry, a few at a time, until the batter is a golden brown. Remove, drain for a moment on absorbent paper and serve immediately.

NIWATORI TO YASAI NO TOGARASHI ITAME (*Sautéed Chicken, Vegetables, and Red Pepper*)

1 lb chicken	2 tablespoons oil
Cornflour	3 tablespoons soy sauce
1 small bamboo shoot	2 tablespoons *mirin*
4–5 large mushrooms	¼ teaspoon white pepper
1-inch piece of fresh ginger root	Monosodium glutamate
2 dried red peppers	

Bone the chicken and cut it into cubes. Dip in cornflour and reserve. Drain the bamboo shoots and slice. Slice the mushrooms. Peel the ginger and mince finely. Chop the red peppers finely. Heat the oil in a frying pan and add the ginger and red peppers, stirring for a moment or two. Almost immediately add the chicken and bamboo shoots and sauté quickly until they begin to brown. Add the soy sauce, *mirin* and pepper and fry for two or three minutes longer. Turn out on a platter and serve immediately.

TORINIKU DANGO NO TERINI (*Chicken Balls in Sauce*)

1 lb minced chicken	2 cups water
1 egg	3 tablespoons soy sauce
2 tablespoons flour	1½ tablespoons *mirin*
Monosodium glutamate	2 teaspoons sugar
1 spring onion	*Sansho* or *shichimi* pepper
½ teaspoon salt	

Mix together the minced chicken, egg, flour, salt and a dash of mono-sodium glutamate. Mince the spring onion and add to the chicken mix-ture, mixing well. Form into small balls and roll in cornflour. Heat the water in a large-bottomed saucepan and when it comes to the boil add the chicken balls, boiling until they are cooked through, about three or four minutes. Add the soy sauce, *mirin* and sugar and cover with a lid. Continue to cook for five or six minutes over a medium heat. Remove and serve with a sprinkling of *sansho* or *shichimi* pepper if available.

TORINIKU NO DANGO (*Chicken Croquettes*)

1 lb minced chicken	1 teaspoon sugar
3 dried mushrooms	½ teaspoon salt
2 spring onions	Monosodium glutamate
1 egg	¼ cup bread crumbs
1 oz carrots	2 sheets laver seaweed, *nori*
1 tablespoon *sake*	(optional)
1 tablespoon light soy sauce	3 tablespoons oil

Soak the dried mushrooms for about fifteen minutes in cold water or until they become soft. Drain and mince. Boil the carrot in salted water until barely tender, drain and mince. Mince the spring onions. Combine these vegetables with the chicken, egg, bread crumbs, *sake*, soy sauce, sugar, salt and monosodium glutamate, and mix well. Form into balls about 1 inch in diameter. Heat the oil in a frying pan and add a few of the balls, frying until well-browned and done. Fry all the balls and arrange on a serving platter. Garnish with a sprinkling of laver seaweed, toasted over a flame until crisp and broken into fragments. If seaweed is not available the croquettes may be rolled in chopped parsley.

NIWATORI TO NIRA NO ITAMEMONO (*Sautéed Chicken and Chives*)

1 lb chicken	2 tablespoons *mirin*
1 bunch chives	¼ teaspoon red pepper
2 tablespoons oil	1 teaspoon sesame seed oil
3 tablespoons soy sauce	

Bone the chicken and cut into cubes. Cut the chives into 1½-inch lengths. Heat the oil in a frying pan and when hot add the chicken, sautéeing quickly. Add the chives and continue to cook over a hot fire for a further minute. Add the seasonings of soy sauce, *mirin*, and red pepper, and cook for two minutes longer. Add the sesame seed oil, cook for a minute, turn out on a platter and serve immediately.

CHICKEN LOAF

1 lb minced chicken	1 tablespoon *sake*
4 dried mushrooms	½ teaspoon salt
3 oz bamboo shoots	1 teaspoon sugar
2 spring onions	¼ teaspoon monosodium glutamate
1 egg	¼ cup fresh bread crumbs
2 tablespoons light soy sauce	2 teaspoons poppy or sesame seeds

Soak the dried mushrooms in water for about fifteen minutes or until they become soft. Drain and chop finely. Mince the bamboo shoots and spring onions. Mix together these minced vegetables with all the other ingredients except the poppy seeds. When all the ingredients are thoroughly worked together put into a baking tin and form the chicken mixture into a loaf about 2 inches high. Sprinkle the poppy seeds over the top and bake in a moderate oven until the loaf is done, about thirty to forty minutes. It may be eaten either hot or cold.

BACON AND CHICKEN ROLLS

1 lb chicken breasts	1 tablespoon sugar
12 slices bacon	1 tablespoon *mirin*
2 tablespoons oil	2 teaspoons *sake*
4 tablespoons soy sauce	

Bone the chicken breasts and remove the skin. Cut the meat into pieces about 2 inches long and 1 inch in diameter. These pieces of chicken breast are sold in every chicken shop in Japan and are called *sasami*. Cut the pieces of bacon in half and wrap a length of bacon around each piece of *sasami*, securing with a toothpick. Heat the oil in a frying pan and add the chicken and bacon rolls, frying until well browned. Pour off the surplus oil. Add the soy sauce, sugar, *mirin* and *sake* and cook for five to ten minutes, until the rolls are well flavoured. Remove, take out the toothpicks, arrange on a serving platter, garnish with parsley and serve.

TORINIKU TO EDO-NEGI (*Sautéed Chicken and Leeks*)

1 lb chicken	3 tablespoons *sake*
Cornflour	2 teaspoons sugar
6–8 leeks	Monosodium glutamate
2 tablespoons oil	*Sansho* or *shichimi* pepper
¼ cup soy sauce	(optional)

Bone the chicken and cut into cubes. Roll the chicken in cornflour. Wash the leeks thoroughly and cut the white part into 1½-inch lengths, discarding the green tops. Heat the oil in a frying pan and when hot add the chicken and leeks, sautéeing quickly until brown. Discard the oil and add the soy sauce, *sake*, sugar and monosodium glutamate, frying for another three or four minutes and shaking the frying pan back and forth to cover the chicken and leeks with the sauce. Sprinkle with a little *sansho* or *shichimi* pepper if available, turn out on a platter and serve immediately.

SAKE CHICKEN

1 lb chicken breasts	1½ tablespoons sugar
½ cup *sake*	2 teaspoons mustard
⅓ cup vinegar	¼ teaspoon monosodium glutamate

Bone the chicken breasts and remove the skin, cutting the meat into pieces about ¾ inch in diameter. Put the chicken into a bowl, pour over the *sake* and marinate for one hour, turning the pieces three or four times. Bring a shallow pan of salted water to the boil and poach the pieces of chicken until just done. They will take not more than three or four minutes each. Do not overcook them or all their flavour will be lost. Remove and drain well. Mix together in a small saucepan the vinegar, sugar, mustard and monosodium glutamate. Bring to the boil and remove from heat. Cool the sauce, pour over the chicken and serve cold.

BEEF TERIYAKI

6 steaks	1 teaspoon ginger juice
4 tablespoons *mirin*	1 clove of garlic
4 tablespoons light soy sauce	1 tablespoon oil

Make a marinade by mixing together the soy sauce, *mirin*, finely-chopped garlic and ginger juice, obtained by grating about 1 inch of fresh ginger root and squeezing out the juice by hand. Marinate the steak in this mixture for thirty minutes. Heat the oil in a frying pan and add the steaks, browning quickly. Pour over the remaining marinade and fry for four or five minutes longer, until the meat has taken on a glazed appearance. This dish is usually garnished with fresh young ginger sprouts, or tiny cucumbers marinated in vinegar and soy sauce.

GYŪNIKU TO YASAI NO ITAMEMONO (*Sautéed Beef with Vegetables*)

1 lb steak	$\frac{1}{4}$ cup cornflour
2 eggs	2 tablespoons oil
2 green peppers	1 teaspoon salt
4 large fresh mushrooms	$\frac{1}{4}$ teaspoon pepper
1 small carrot	$\frac{1}{4}$ teaspoon monosodium glutamate
2 oz fresh bean sprouts (optional)	2 tablepoons soy sauce

Beat the eggs and fry them into a thin omelet. Cut into thin strips about 1 inch long and reserve. Remove the seeds, stems and membranes from the green peppers and cut lengthwise into eights. Slice the steak into strips, $\frac{1}{4}$ inch by 1 inch by 2 inches. Slice both the carrot and mushrooms into thin strips, not more than $\frac{1}{8}$ inch thick. Wash the bean sprouts and drain. Salt the steak slices and roll in the cornflour. Heat the oil in a frying pan, add the steak and sauté quickly, until brown. Remove to a platter and keep warm. Add all the vegetables, sprinkle with salt and pepper and fry until they begin to brown. Add the meat and soy sauce, cook for a further minute or two and then turn out on a serving plate. Garnish with the omelet strips and serve immediately.

GYŪNIKU NO KUSHIYAKI (Beef and Onion Kebabs)

1 lb beef

2 onions

⅓ cup soy sauce

1 tablespoon *mirin*

2 teaspoons sugar

⅓ cup flour

1 egg, beaten with 1 tablespoon water

1 cup fine bread crumbs

1 pint or more of oil

Cut the beef into 1-inch cubes. Peel the onions and cut them into pieces about the same size as the beef. Arrange the beef and onions on oiled metal or bamboo skewers. Mix together the soy sauce, *mirin* and sugar and marinate the kebabs in this mixture for one hour, turning frequently. Drain well. Dip the kebabs in flour, then the beaten egg, then the bread crumbs. They can then be set aside for a wait of anything up to two hours before cooking.

Heat the oil in a deep pan. When it reaches a temperature of 340° to 355° F. (see pages 87–88) put a few of the kebabs into the oil and fry until golden brown. Remove, drain for a moment or two on absorbent paper and serve immediately.

GYŪNIKU NO YAWATAMAKI (Beef and Burdock Rolls)

1 lb beef

4 burdock roots

1 tablespoon vinegar

3 tablespoons oil

4 tablespoons soy sauce

1 tablespoon sugar

1 tablespoon *mirin*

2 teaspoons *sake*

Have the beef sliced very thin, as for *sukiyaki*. With the back of a knife scrape off the skin of the burdock roots. Cut them into lengths the same as the width of the beef slices. Submerge the burdock root in cold water to prevent discoloration. Bring a saucepan of water to the boil and add the vinegar and burdock root, boiling for three or four minutes. Remove and drain.

Lay out the slices of beef and put a length of burdock root in the centre of each piece, rolling the beef tightly around it and securing the rolls with a toothpick or two. Heat the oil in a frying pan, add the beef rolls and brown. When the rolls are well browned, add the soy sauce, sugar, *mirin* and *sake* and continue to cook for five or ten minutes, until the rolls are well-flavoured. Remove, take out the toothpick, cut into 2-inch lengths and serve, hot or cold.

GYŪNIKU NO AMIYAKI (Sautéed Steak with Sesame Seeds)

6 steaks
2 tablespoons white sesame seeds
1 clove of garlic
2 spring onions
2 tablespoons soy sauce
1 tablespoon *sake*
1 teaspoon sugar

DIPPING SAUCE
½ cup light soy sauce
¼ cup *dashi* or other stock
¼ teaspoon red pepper
1-inch piece of fresh ginger root

Chop the spring onion and garlic finely and mix together with the soy sauce, *sake* and sugar. Toast the sesame seeds in a dry frying pan until they begin to jump. Remove and put in a *suribachi* or mortar, or through a nut chopper, crushing them roughly to release their flavour. Add the crushed seeds to the marinade sauce. Add the steaks and marinate for twenty minutes, turning frequently and making sure that the meat is well covered with the liquid.

Make a dipping sauce by mixing together the soy sauce, *dashi*, red pepper and a little grated ginger. Pour into individual sauce dishes.

Drain the meat and grill it to the desired degree, preferably over charcoal. Serve immediately, accompanied by the bowls of dipping sauce.

LAMB KEBABS

1 lb lamb chops, without bones
2 cloves of garlic
1-inch piece of fresh ginger root
    (optional)
¼ teaspoon red pepper
¼ teaspoon black pepper
Monosodium glutamate

½ cup light soy sauce
¼ cup *mirin*
1 tablespoon sugar
4 leeks
1 onion
2 green peppers

Cut the lamb into cubes about ¾ inch square. Clean the leeks carefully
and cut into 1-inch lengths, using the white part only. Cut both the
green peppers and onion into pieces about the same size as the lamb.
Chop the garlic and ginger finely and put in a small saucepan with the
soy sauce, *mirin*, sugar, pepper and a dash of monosodium glutamate.
When the sauce comes to the boil remove, pour over the lamb and allow
it to marinate for thirty minutes. Arrange the lamb and vegetables on
metal or bamboo skewers and grill under a hot grill or over charcoal.
Turn once during the cooking and baste three or four times with the
marinade.

BRAISED LAMB WITH VEGETABLES

1 lb lamb
4 spring onions
3 green peppers
¼ cup light soy sauce
2 tablespoons *mirin*

1 tablespoon vinegar
¼ teaspoon red pepper
1 teaspoon grated lemon peel
1 clove of garlic
1 tablespoon oil

Slice the lamb into thin pieces, no thicker than ¼ inch. Cut the spring
onions, including green tops, diagonally into ½-inch widths. Remove the
seeds, stems and membranes from the green peppers and cut lengthwise into quarters or eighths. Chop the garlic finely. Heat the oil in a
frying pan and add the chopped garlic and lamb. Fry for a minute or
two, then add the green peppers and spring onions. Fry for another minute
and add the seasonings of soy sauce, *mirin*, vinegar, red pepper and
lemon peel. Cook for three or four minutes longer, remove to a serving
dish and serve immediately.

BUTANIKU TSUKEYAKI (*Sautéed Pork and Vegetables*)

3 tablespoons white sesame seeds
1 clove of garlic
1-inch piece of fresh ginger root
6 lean pork cutlets
Salt
Pepper
Monosodium glutamate
4 tablespoons *sake*

4 tablespoons soy sauce
1 tablespoon sugar
3 oz chrysanthemum leaves
(optional)
4 spring onions
1 small carrot
2 tablespoons oil

Toast the sesame seeds in a dry frying pan until they begin to jump. Stir constantly to prevent them from burning. Remove from the fire, and in a *suribachi* or mortar crush them roughly to release their flavour. Mince the ginger and garlic. Put in a bowl the sesame seeds, ginger and garlic along with the *sake*, sugar and soy sauce. Marinate the pork in this mixture for ten to fifteen minutes. Heat the oil in a frying pan and when hot add the pork cutlets, frying quickly. Sprinkle lightly with salt, pepper and monosodium glutamate. When the pork is done remove to a platter and keep warm. Put in the frying pan the spring onions, sliced diagonally in ¼-inch widths, the carrots cut into thin strips, and the chrysanthemum leaves. Fry for four or five minutes, then add the remaining marinade. Cook for a further minute. Surround the meat with the cooked vegetables and serve immediately.

YUDEBUTA (*Boiled Tenderloin of Pork*)

1 tenderloin of pork
1½ quarts water
½ cup soy sauce
2-inch piece of fresh ginger root

2 spring onions
¼ teaspoon monosodium glutamate
Mustard

Bring the water to the boil and add the soy sauce, monosodium glutamate, the ginger, peeled and sliced, and the spring onions, roughly chopped. Add the tenderloin, bring to the boil again and simmer until the pork is done. This will take only twenty to thirty minutes. Let the tenderloin cool slightly in the stock, then remove and drain. Slice and eat cold with a little mustard. This is a simple dish, but delicious as a cold cut or in sandwiches.

PORK AND BAMBOO SHOOTS

1 lb lean pork   2 tablespoons *sake*
2 small bamboo shoots   1 teaspoon sugar
½ cup green peas   ¼ teaspoon red pepper
2 tablespoons oil   ¼ teaspoon monosodium glutamate
4 tablespoons light soy sauce

Cut the pork into ¾-inch cubes. Drain the bamboo shoots and cut into
slices about ¼ inch thick. Heat the oil in a frying pan and add the pork
and bamboo shoots, frying for three or four minutes over a hot flame.
Add the soy sauce, *sake*, sugar, red pepper and monosodium glutamate
and cook for a further five minutes. Add the peas which have already
been boiled and cook for a further minute, until they are just warmed
through. Remove from the fire, turn out on a serving plate and serve
immediately.

BUTANIKU NO MISOITAME (*Pork with Bean Curd*)

1 lb pork   1 oz red bean paste, *aka-miso*
1 bamboo shoot   1 cup *dashi* or chicken stock
6 fresh mushrooms   2 tablespoons *mirin*
1 piece bean curd, *tōfu* (about 1 lb)   ¼ teaspoon red pepper
2–3 tablespoons oil   ¼ teaspoon monosodium glutamate

Cut the pork into cubes about 1 inch square. Drain the bamboo shoot
and slice. Wash the mushrooms, remove any hard bits of stem and
slice. Wrap the bean curd in a clean cloth and press firmly to remove
some of its water. Cut the bean curd into cubes. Heat the oil in a frying
pan and add the pork and bamboo shoots, sautéeing until they begin to
brown. Add the mushrooms and bean curd and sauté for two or three
minutes longer. The bean curd will break into small pieces but this does
not matter. Mix together the *dashi* or chicken stock, bean paste, *mirin*,
red pepper and monosodium glutamate and pour it over the meat and
vegetables. Mix well and continue to cook for three or four minutes
longer. Remove to a bowl and serve immediately. This recipe calls for
neither salt nor soy sauce, because red bean paste is very salty and
contains enough for the entire dish.

BUTANIKU TO RINGO NO DANGO (*Pork and Apple Balls*)

1 lb minced pork
3 dried mushrooms
½ apple
1 egg
¼ cup bread crumbs
1 spring onion
1 tablespoon *sake*
1 teaspoon salt
¼ teaspoon pepper

¼ teaspoon monosodium glutamate
⅓ cup cornflour
1 pint or more of vegetable oil

SAUCE SANBAIZU
½ cup light soy sauce
½ cup vinegar
1½ tablespoons sugar
¼ teaspoon monosodium glutamate

Soak the dried mushrooms in cold water until soft and dice into tiny cubes. Peel the apple and dice in the same way as the mushrooms. Combine with the pork, egg, minced spring onion, *sake*, bread crumbs, salt, pepper and monosodium glutamate. When all the ingredients are thoroughly mixed together form into balls, about 1 inch in diameter. Roll in the cornflour. Heat the oil and fry the balls a few at a time until well browned. Serve with the *sanbaizu* sauce, made by combining the soy sauce, vinegar, sugar and monosodium glutamate. A little mustard may also be added if desired.

BUTANIKU NO DANGO (*Pork Balls*)

1 lb minced pork
3 dried mushrooms
2 spring onions
1 egg
¼ cup bread crumbs
1 tablespoon soy sauce
½ teaspoon salt
1 teaspoon sugar
3 tablespoons oil

DIPPING SAUCE
⅓ cup *sake*
⅓ cup light soy sauce
3 tablespoons vinegar
1 tablespoon sugar
2 red peppers
¼ cup *dashi* broth

Soak the mushrooms in cold water until they soften; drain and chop finely. Mince the spring onions. Combine the minced vegetables with the pork, egg, bread crumbs, soy sauce, salt and sugar and mix thoroughly.

Form into balls about 1 inch in diameter. Heat the oil in a frying pan and fry until the meat balls are well browned.

Make a dipping sauce by slicing two red peppers into fine rings and mixing with the *sake*, soy sauce, vinegar, sugar and *dashi*. Serve the meat balls hot with individual bowls of this sauce.

PORK WITH MUSTARD SAUCE

6 lean pork cutlets	3 tablespoons light soy sauce
1 tablespoon oil	2 teaspoons sugar
2 tablespoons white sesame seeds	1 tablespoon mustard
3 tablespoons *sake*	1 spring onion

Heat a little oil in a frying pan, add the pork cutlets and brown quickly. Add the *sake*, soy sauce, sugar and sesame seeds, which have been toasted in a dry frying pan and crushed in a *suribachi* or mortar. Turn down the fire and cook for four or five minutes. Mix the mustard to a paste with a little water and add to the pork. Cook for two or three minutes longer. Arrange the cutlets on a serving platter, pour the sauce over the top and garnish with finely-chopped spring onion.

PORK AND ONION STEW

1 lb lean pork	1 teaspoon salt
1 lb onions	1 tablespoon *sake*
2 tablespoons oil	¼ teaspoon monosodium glutamate
2 cups *dashi* or chicken stock	¼ teaspoon pepper
2 tablespoons soy sauce	1 tablespoon flour
2 teaspoons sugar	½ cup green peas

Slice the pork into six cutlets. Chop the onions roughly, or slice into rings. Heat the oil in a frying pan, add the pork and onions and fry over a hot fire until they begin to brown. Add the stock, soy sauce, sugar, *sake*, pepper and monosodium glutamate. Bring to the boil, lower the heat and simmer for fifteen minutes. Dissolve the cornflour in a little cold water and add to the stew, boiling until the sauce thickens slightly. Add the green peas and cook for a moment or two longer. Remove to a serving dish and serve with hot boiled rice.

BUTA KUSHIKATSU (*Pork Kebabs*)

1 lb lean pork, preferably fillet	¼ cup flour
6 leeks	1 egg, beaten with 1 tablespoon
4 green peppers	water
Salt	1 cup fresh bread crumbs
Pepper	1 pint or more of vegetable oil
Monosodium glutamate	

Cut the pork into cubes about 1 inch square. Clean the leeks and green peppers and cut into pieces about the same size as the pork. Arrange the pork and vegetables on oiled bamboo or metal skewers, beginning and ending with a piece of pork. Sprinkle the skewered meat and vegetables with salt, pepper and monosodium glutamate. Dip the kebabs in flour, then into the beaten egg mixture, then into the bread crumbs. These can then be set aside for a wait of anything up to two hours before frying.

Heat the oil in a deep pan. When the oil temperature is 355° F (*see* directions for cooking *tempura*, pages 87–88) put the kebabs into the oil, a few at a time, and fry until golden brown on the outside and the pork is done. Serve immediately, with hot Chinese mustard if desired.

BUTANIKU TO HARUSAME NO SUNOMONO (*Chilled Pork and Noodles*)

8 oz lean pork	4 spring onions
2 tablespoons soy sauce	1-inch piece of fresh ginger root
¼ teaspoon pepper	¼ cup light soy sauce
Cornflour	¼ cup vinegar
4 oz dried *harusame* noodles	2 teaspoons sesame seed oil
1 cucumber	¼ teaspoon monosodium glutamate

Cut the pork into thin strips, about ¼ inch thick, ½ inch wide and 2 inches long. Sprinkle these strips with the soy sauce and pepper and let them marinate for twenty minutes. Bring a saucepan of water to the boil. Drain the pork slices, roll in cornflour and cook by dipping into the boiling water until done. This will take only a few seconds for each piece. Drain the pork slices and reserve.

Cook the noodles in a large pan of salted boiling water. They cook in a very short time, four or five minutes, and when done are translucent. Remove, drain and rinse in cold water.

Cut the cucumber into julienne strips, salt lightly and allow to stand for thirty minutes. Drain off the excess water and dry with a clean cloth. Peel and grate the ginger and mix together with the soy sauce, vinegar, sesame seed oil and monosodium glutamate. Put the noodles, pork and cucumbers in a bowl, pour the dressing over the top and toss until the ingredients are well covered with the dressing. Garnish with the finely sliced spring onions and serve.

SHINJAGAIMO TO BUTANIKU NO NITSUKE
(Pork and New Potatoes)

1 lb new potatoes	1–2 tablespoons sugar
1 lb lean pork	¼ teaspoon monosodium glutamate
3 cups *dashi* or chicken broth	1-inch piece of fresh ginger root
½ cup light soy sauce	

Scrub the potatoes thoroughly. Cut the pork into cubes, 1 to 1½ inches square. Put the broth and potatoes into a saucepan and bring to the boil. When it begins to boil add the pork and simmer for ten minutes. Add the soy sauce, sugar, monosodium glutamate and simmer for a further fifteen minutes. Remove from the broth, turn out into a bowl, garnish with the ginger cut in fine strips and serve at once. The broth may be drunk as a soup.

GYŪ-REBĀ NO ITAMENI (Sautéed Liver)

1 lb beef or calves liver	2 tablespoons oil
2 tablespoons soy sauce	¼ teaspoon red pepper
2 tablespoons *mirin*	3 tablespoons dark soy sauce
½ teaspoon salt	1 teaspoon sugar
4 spring onions	Monosodium glutamate
1 clove of garlic	1 teaspoon sesame seed oil
1-inch piece of fresh ginger root	

Sprinkle the sliced liver with a little salt, soy sauce and *mirin* and let marinate thirty minutes. Chop the spring onions roughly and mince the garlic and ginger. Heat the oil in a frying pan and add the liver, sautée-ing quickly until brown. Remove and keep warm. Put the chopped onions, garlic, ginger and red pepper in the frying pan and cook for a minute or two. Add the liver, soy sauce, sugar and a dash of mono-sodium glutamate and fry for a further two or three minutes. Add the sesame seed oil. Turn out on a platter and serve immediately.

KIMO NO IRITSUKE (*Sautéed Chicken Livers*)

1 lb chicken livers	$\frac{1}{4}$ teaspoon monosodium glutamate
1 clove of garlic	$\frac{1}{4}$ teaspoon pepper
1-inch piece of ginger root	2 tablespoons oil
3 tablespoons light soy sauce	1 teaspoon cornflour
2 tablespoons *mirin*	

Clean the livers carefully and cut in halves. Mix together the garlic, grated, the soy sauce and the *mirin*. Grate the ginger and squeeze the juice into the marinade. Marinate the livers in this mixture for fifteen minutes. Remove the livers and drain, reserving the marinade. Heat the oil in a frying pan and add the livers, sautéeing quickly until brown. Dissolve the cornflour in a little cold water and add to the marinade. Pour the marinade into the frying pan and cook over a medium heat for three or four minutes, until the sauce has thickened slightly. Remove to a serving plate and serve immediately.

KIMO NO TSUKEAGE (*Deep-fried Chicken Livers*)

1 lb chicken livers	2 tablespoons *sake*
1-inch piece of fresh ginger root	2 tablespoons cornflour
2 tablespoons soy sauce	1 pint or more of vegetable oil

Clean the livers carefully and cut into slices $\frac{1}{4}$ inch thick. Mix together the soy sauce and *sake*. Grate the ginger and squeeze a little of the juice into the soy sauce and *sake* mixture. Marinate the livers in this mixture for thirty minutes. Sprinkle the cornflour over the top of the marinating livers and mix, covering the livers with a kind of batter made from the cornflour and marinade. Heat the oil in a deep saucepan to a temperature of 355° F and drop in spoonfuls of the livers, a few at a time, frying until brown.

VEGETABLES AND SALADS

In my begging bowl
Violets and dandelions
Are mixed together:
To the Buddhas of the Three Worlds
I shall offer them.
   RYŌKAN

Strict Buddhist doctrine of course implies vegetarianism, though from
the earliest days there were many lapses on the part of ordinary people
and of priests also. Since it was thought less wicked to eat fish than to
eat meat, wild boar was referred to euphemistically as 'mountain whale',
the mammalian status of the whale being, ironically, overlooked.

Nowadays comparatively few even among Buddhist priests follow a
completely vegetarian diet, though the Tendai sect and certain branches
of Zen and Shingon still enjoin vegetarianism quite strictly. We have a
pleasant memory of entertaining two Zen monks who consumed vast
numbers of ham sandwiches while happily explaining that since they
were outside the monastery the rules no longer applied.

In spite of all these lapses from Buddhist grace, the Japanese people
nevertheless, for the most part, eat far more vegetables and far less flesh
and fowl than we do in the West. Doctrinal considerations aside, the
superb quality and great variety of vegetables sold in Japan would more
than justify such habits. The visitor from the West can scarcely fail to
wonder at radishes 18 inches long and as thick as a man's arm; splen-
didly tight and crisp Chinese cabbages, huge tomatoes and mushrooms,
and a whole range of other specialities. So scrubbed and clean, so

trimmed and perfect are they that every little local greengrocer's looks like the tableau of winning entries at a western agricultural show or county fair.

In order fully to understand the place of vegetables in Japanese food it is necessary to bear in mind first that the conventional western distinction between fresh salads and cooked vegetables is largely ignored in the Japanese cuisine. There are two main reasons for this. First, when vegetables are cooked at all in Japan they are usually cooked very briefly, in a way very similar to the Chinese practice. Secondly, even cooked vegetables are quite often eaten cold, and the resulting dish is much more like what we should call a salad than the 'two veg' of a western dinner.

The other important point to remember is that it is comparatively rare for a vegetable to be served plain. Apart from rice, which is habitually eaten in this way, vegetables are generally mixed, in combination with others, or with fish, meat, bean curd, bean paste and so forth. This practice, in spite of the simplicity of materials, produces a complexity of flavours in which much of the attraction of the Japanese cuisine is to be found.

DAIKON NAMASU (*Radish and Carrot Salad*)

10 oz Japanese radish, *daikon*	2 tablespoons sugar
5 oz carrot	1 tablespoon light soy sauce
1 teaspoon salt	½ teaspoon monosodium glutamate
½ cup vinegar	

Peel the radish and scrape the carrot and cut both into julienne strips. Salt lightly and allow to stand for thirty minutes. Press out the excess water with the hands, or pat dry with a clean cloth. Mix together the vinegar, sugar, soy sauce and monosodium glutamate. Put the radish and carrot strips in a salad bowl, pour the dressing over them, mix lightly and serve.

RED CAVIAR AND RADISH SALAD

6 oz red caviar	1½ tablespoons light soy sauce
10 oz Japanese radish, *daikon*	Monosodium glutamate
3 tablespoons vinegar	

Peel the radish and grate, draining away the juice. If a great deal of moisture seems to be left in the radish, squeeze it out by hand. Pile the radish on a serving plate and put the caviar on top. Mix together the vinegar, soy sauce and a dash of monosodium glutamate and pour over the caviar and radish. Garnish with a sprig of greenery.

SALMON AND RADISH SALAD

This is a very common lunch-time snack as well as a salad used in more elaborate dinners.

1 8-oz tin of salmon	1 teaspoon salt
10 oz Japanese radish, *daikon*	1 teaspoon sugar
¼ teaspoon red pepper	Monosodium glutamate
2 tablespoons vinegar	

Drain the juice from the salmon and arrange on a plate. Peel the radish and grate, draining away the juice. Add the vinegar, red pepper, salt, sugar and a dash of monosodium glutamate to the radish and mix. Pile the radish around the perimeter of the salmon and serve.

COD ROE AND RADISH SALAD

6 oz cod roe	4 tablespoons vinegar
2 tablespoons soy sauce	1 tablespoon *mirin*
1 tablespoon *sake*	Monosodium glutamate
10 oz Japanese radish, *daikon*	½ teaspoon salt

Wash the roes thoroughly. Mix together the soy sauce and *sake* and pour over the roes, letting them marinate in the mixture for thirty minutes. Remove the skin of the roe if it has not already been removed. Peel the radish and grate finely. Drain away as much of the juice as possible, squeezing out the remaining juice by hand. Mix together the vinegar, *mirin*, salt and a little monosodium glutamate, and pour over the radish, mixing well. Break the roes into pieces, mix gently with the radish and serve.

KYURIMOMI (*Cucumber Salad*)

1 cucumber	2 tablespoons sugar
1 tablespoon white sesame seeds	2 tablespoons light soy sauce
1 teaspoon salt	½ teaspoon monosodium glutamate
½ cup vinegar	

Wash the cucumber and slice without peeling into paper-thin rounds. Salt lightly and put in a colander. Place a bowl or plate on top of the cucumbers in order to press out some of the liquid. Let stand for thirty minutes. Pat the cucumbers dry with a clean cloth. Mix together the vinegar, sugar, soy sauce and monosodium glutamate, pour over the cucumbers and mix lightly. Toast the sesame seeds in a dry frying pan, stirring constantly until they begin to jump. Remove from the fire and crush in a *suribachi* or mortar. Sprinkle over the cucumbers and serve.

CUCUMBER AND CRAB SALAD

1 cucumber	2 tablespoons sugar
8 oz crab	½ teaspoon monosodium glutamate
½ cup vinegar	1-inch piece of fresh ginger root
½ teaspoon salt	(optional)
1 tablespoon light soy sauce	

Prepare the cucumber as in the recipe above. Break the crab into small pieces, making sure there are no fragments of shell remaining. Mix together the vinegar, salt, soy sauce, sugar and monosodium glutamate. Put the cucumber and crab in a salad bowl, pour the dressing over the top and mix well. Let them marinate until time to serve, then drain away excess dressing. If desired, the dish may be garnished with fresh ginger root, peeled and sliced into fine strips.

CUCUMBER AND SEAWEED SALAD

3½ oz *wakame* seaweed	2 teaspoons sugar
1 cucumber	Salt
4 tablespoons vinegar	Monosodium glutamate
3 tablespoons dark soy sauce	

Soak the *wakame* seaweed in water until it becomes tender. If it is young, fresh *wakame* this will take about ten minutes; if older, it will take perhaps twenty to thirty minutes. Cut the cucumber into thin slices, salt lightly and let stand for thirty minutes. Pat dry with a clean cloth. Cut the *wakame* into 1½-inch lengths. Mix together the vinegar, soy sauce, sugar, salt and a dash of monosodium glutamate. Combine the cucumber and *wakame* in a salad bowl. Pour the vinegar dressing over it, mix gently and serve.

CUCUMBER AND SHRIMP SALAD

1 cucumber	2 teaspoons sugar
8 oz shrimp	½ teaspoon monosodium glutamate
½ cup vinegar	1-inch piece of fresh ginger root
1 teaspoon salt	(optional)

Wash the cucumber and slice into julienne strips. Salt lightly and let stand in a colander for thirty minutes. Press out the excess liquid with a dry, clean cloth. Use either tinned or fresh shrimp; if fresh shrimp are used, cook by immersing in salted boiling water for one or two minutes. Cool and remove shells. Mix together the vinegar, salt, sugar and monosodium glutamate and pour over the shrimp and cucumber strips. Let marinate in this liquid until time to serve and drain before serving. A garnish of finely-sliced ginger root may be added if desired.

CUCUMBER AND RAW FISH SALAD

8 oz mackerel, herrings, or sprats	1 tablespoon light soy sauce
8 oz cucumber	1 tablespoon sugar
Vinegar, about 1 cup	2 teaspoons *mirin*
Salt	1 tablespoon Japanese horseradish,
Monosodium glutamate	*wasabi*
3 tablespoons vinegar	

Fillet the fish and salt, rather heavily, on the skin side. Allow to stand for twenty minutes. When the salt has melted and the surface of the fish

5

becomes damp, put it in a shallow pan and cover with vinegar. Let stand for fifteen minutes or until the flesh has become firm. Remove the skin and cut into bite-size pieces. Wash the cucumber and, without peeling, cut into julienne strips. Salt lightly and allow to stand for twenty minutes. Dry with a clean cloth.

Prepare the dressing by mixing together the vinegar, soy sauce, sugar, *mirin* and a dash of monosodium glutamate. Arrange the fish and cucumbers in individual salad bowls and pour the dressing over the top. If desired, this dish may be garnished with a little Japanese horseradish which has been mixed to mustard-like consistency with a little water.

CUCUMBER AND CHICKEN SALAD

8 oz boned chicken breast	½ teaspoon salt
1 cucumber	1½ tablespoons soy sauce
½ cup vinegar	1 tablespoon Japanese horseradish,
¼ teaspoon monosodium glutamate	*wasabi*

Cut the chicken into thin slices about 1 inch long and ¼ inch thick. Dip into boiling water and remove after a few seconds taking care not to overcook. Drain well and sprinkle with a little vinegar. Cut the cucumber diagonally in thin slices and cut these slices into narrow strips. Sprinkle with salt and let stand for thirty minutes. Dry them with a clean cloth. Mix the *wasabi* with water until it is the consistency of mustard and add the soy sauce and monosodium glutamate. Put the chicken and cucumber in a bowl, pour the dressing over the top and mix gertly.

KYŪRI NO MISOAE (*Cucumbers with Bean Paste Dressing*)

1 cucumber	2 tablespoons *mirin*
Salt	¼ teaspoon monosodium glutamate
½ cup red bean paste, *aka-miso*	

Wash the cucumber. Bring a saucepan of water to the boil and dip the cucumber in it, removing almost immediately and rinsing under cold running water. This will turn the cucumber a vivid green. Slice into rounds and sprinkle with salt. Let stand for thirty minutes. In the meantime mix the bean paste with the *mirin* and monosodium glutamate. Dry the cucumber with a clean kitchen towel. To serve, either mix the cucumber slices with the bean paste or arrange on tiny individual plates a small mound of cucumber with a smaller mound of the bean paste dressing placed next to it.

POTATO SALAD

1 lb potatoes
A few *mitsuba* leaves or a small
    bunch of parsley
1 tablespoon black sesame seeds
½ cup vinegar

1 tablespoon *mirin*
1 tablespoon sugar
1 teaspoon salt
1 teaspoon light soy sauce
¼ teaspoon monosodium glutamate

Peel the potatoes and cut into julienne strips. Drop into boiling salted water and cook until tender, no more than thirty to forty seconds. Take care not to overcook or they will become mushy. Drain well and sprinkle with salt. Chop the *mitsuba* leaves or parsley finely and gently mix in with the potatoes. Parch the sesame seeds in a dry frying pan until they begin to jump, stirring slowly so that they won't burn. Remove, and reserve. In a small saucepan mix together the remaining ingredients and bring to the boil, stirring until the sugar is dissolved. Remove from the fire, cool slightly and pour over the warm potatoes. Allow them to marinate a few minutes. Arrange the potatoes in a serving dish, sprinkle the sesame seeds over the top and serve.

FRESH ASPARAGUS SALAD

1 lb fresh asparagus
⅓ cup light soy sauce

¼ teaspoon red pepper

Clean the asparagus and boil for six to ten minutes in salted water until the stalks are just tender. Drain well. Mix together the soy sauce and red pepper. Arrange the asparagus stalks on a platter, pour the dressing over them and serve.

BROCCOLI SALAD WITH GOLDEN DRESSING

2 bunches broccoli
3 oz Japanese radish, *daikon*, or
   a few red radishes
Salt

KIMIZU DRESSING
3 egg yolks
¾ cup cold water
2 tablespoons sugar
3 tablespoons vinegar
1 tablespoon cornflour
3 teaspoons Japanese horseradish,
   wasabi

Cut the broccoli flowerlets off the stalks. Bring a saucepan of salted water to the boil and drop in the flowerlets for thirty to forty seconds. Do not cook longer or they will lose their bright green colour. Remove from the water, drain and chill. Slice the *daikon* or red radishes into paper-thin slices. Arrange the broccoli on a plate and distribute the radish slices over the top. Make the *kimizu* dressing according to the recipe on page 134; chill and spoon over the top or around the sides of the broccoli.

CELERY, CUCUMBER, AND SCALLOP SALAD WITH GOLDEN DRESSING

This salad is essentially the same as the combination salad on page 134 except that scallops are substituted for the chicken and the tomatoes are omitted. Prepare the celery and cucumbers as in that recipe. Boil about 6 oz scallops in salted water until they are tender. Remove, drain, and cut each scallop into three or four pieces. Arrange the vegetables and fish in a shallow bowl and cover with *kimizu* dressing (*see* page 134).

CHRYSANTHEMUM TURNIPS

10 small turnips
1 teaspoon salt
½ cup vinegar
½ teaspoon salt
1 tablespoon *mirin*

1 or 2 red peppers
¼ teaspoon monosodium glutamate
10 chrysanthemum leaves
   (optional)

Select small, well-shaped turnips, and wash and peel. Cut them in the style the Japanese call the chrysanthemum cut. You do this by slicing about seven-eighths of the way through the turnip in a fine checker-board pattern leaving the bottom intact. If necessary slice a small piece off the bottom so that the turnip will sit squarely on a plate. Sprinkle with salt and allow to stand for thirty minutes. Squeeze out excess water with a clean dry cloth. Mix together the vinegar, salt, *mirin* and mono-sodium glutamate and bring to the boil. Remove and add thinly sliced red peppers. Pour this dressing over the turnips and leave them to marinate in this dressing until it is time to serve. Sometimes a little red colouring is added to one-half of the dressing, and half the turnips are dyed pink. Garnish with the chrysanthemum leaves.

APPLE AND SPINACH SALAD WITH SESAME SEEDS

1 lb fresh spinach	3 tablespoons white sesame seeds
1 apple	1 tablespoon sugar
3 tablespoons light soy sauce	Monosodium glutamate

Wash the spinach and do not remove stems unless they are very tough. Tie the spinach together in a neat bundle so that the stems and leaves are all pointing in the same direction. Bring a large kettle of salted water to the boil and add the spinach, pushing it under the surface of the water. Let the water come to the boil again and allow the spinach to cook one or two minutes. If it cooks too long its fresh green colour will be lost. Remove, drain and cool quickly, squeezing out the excess water with your hands. The spinach should now form a neat, bright-green cylinder.

Peel the apple and cut it into small pieces. Allow to stand for five minutes in slightly salted cold water. Toast the sesame seeds in a dry frying pan, stirring constantly. Remove from the fire when they begin to jump, crush in a *suribachi* or mortar, or by putting through a nut grinder. Mix the sesame seeds with the soy sauce, sugar and mono-sodium glutamate.

Cut the spinach into 1-inch lengths. Drain the apples and add to the spinach. Pour the sesame seed dressing over the top, mix gently and serve.

COMBINATION SALAD WITH GOLDEN DRESSING

This salad uses the *kimizu* dressing, a fluffy, golden mixture which looks like mayonnaise but is much lighter because of the absence of oil.

2 boned breasts of chicken
2 tablespoons cornflour
1 stalk celery
1 cucumber
2–3 tomatoes
Salt

KIMIZU DRESSING
3 egg yolks
¾ cup cold water
2 tablespoons sugar
3 tablespoons vinegar
1 tablespoon cornflour
3 teaspoons Japanese horseradish, *wasabi*

Cut the chicken into bite-size cubes, sprinkle with salt and roll in cornflour. Dip briefly into boiling water until done. Cut the celery into 1¼-inch lengths, then into julienne strips. Cut the cucumber into julienne strips of the same size and allow to stand in cold water until crisp. Dip the tomatoes into boiling water and remove skins, then cut into quarters. To make the dressing, put all the ingredients into a bowl and beat until smooth, or put into a blender and blend for thirty seconds. Pour into the top of a double boiler and cook over simmering water, stirring constantly, until the mixture thickens. This will take only five or six minutes. Stir in the horseradish and cool the dressing. Arrange the vegetables in separate sections in a salad bowl, salt and spoon the dressing over the top.

AUTUMN SALAD

This salad, with its muted colours, is meant to suggest the autumn colouring of the changing leaves.

½ lb Japanese radish, *daikon*
1 small carrot
½ cucumber
2–3 dried mushrooms
½ lb shrimp

3 eggs
2 teaspoons salt
Monosodium glutamate
1 cup vinegar
3 teaspoons sugar

Place the dried mushrooms into cold water to soften. Peel the radish and carrot and slice into thin strips about 1½ inches long. Without peeling, slice the cucumber into similar strips. Salt the vegetables and allow to stand for thirty minutes. Drain the vegetables and pat dry with a clean cloth. Put into a bowl and pour over ¾ of a cup of the vinegar and sprinkle on 2 teaspoons sugar. Put aside in a cold place.

Beat the eggs well, add salt and one teaspoon sugar and a dash of monosodium glutamate. Heat a little oil in a frying pan, add the eggs and scramble over low heat, stirring constantly with a fork or chopsticks. The object is to finish with a dry, finely-granulated mixture, so they should be cooked far longer than one normally cooks scrambled eggs. If still not sufficiently granulated when you remove them from the fire, chop with a knife. Put the eggs into a bowl, add a ¼ cup of vinegar, mix gently and allow to stand for a few minutes. Clean the shrimp and boil briefly until pink, or use tinned shrimp. Drain the vegetables of their vinegar and mix gently with the eggs and shrimp. Taste for seasoning and add more salt, monosodium glutamate, or vinegar as needed. Turn out into a shallow bowl and serve.

SHIRO-AE (*White Salad*)

1 carrot	2 tablespoons light soy sauce
1 block *konnyaku*	Salt
1 piece bean curd, *tōfu* (about 1 lb)	Monosodium glutamate
½ cup white sesame seeds	1 sheet laver seaweed, *nori*
2–3 tablespoons sugar	(optional)

Scrape the carrot and cut into thin slices. Break the *konnyaku* into bite-size pieces and boil in salted water for five minutes. Drain and reserve. Wrap the bean curd in a dry clean cloth and press gently to remove moisture. Toast the seasame seeds in a dry frying pan, stirring constantly, until they begin to jump. Crush the seeds in a *suribachi* or mortar, or put them through a nut grinder. Add the sesame seeds, sugar, soy sauce, salt and monosodium glutamate to the bean curd and mix well. Put the *konnyaku* and carrots in a bowl, pour the sauce over them and mix gently. If desired, the dish may be garnished just before serving with strips of seaweed. Toast the seaweed by passing it back and forth over a gas flame until quite dry, then cut into fine strips.

LOTUS ROOT SALAD

1 lotus root	¼ cup water
1 tablespoon vinegar	½ teaspoon salt
½ cup *sake*	¼ teaspoon monosodium glutamate
4 tablespoons sugar	2 red peppers (optional)

Clean and peel the lotus root and cut it into slices about ⅛ inch thick. Put immediately into cold water to which a little vinegar has been added. This will prevent discoloration. Put the lotus root slices with the vinegared water into a small saucepan and bring to the boil. Cook for two or three minutes, until the slices are tender but still crisp. Remove from the fire and drain. Put the *sake*, sugar, water, salt and monosodium glutamate into a saucepan and bring to the boil. When the sugar has dissolved remove from the fire and pour over the lotus root slices. Allow to stand for twenty minutes. Drain. Chill the lotus root slices and serve. If desired, garnish with thinly sliced rings of red pepper.

BAMBOO SHOOT SALAD

1 bamboo shoot	½ teaspoon salt
4 tablespoons vinegar	¼ teaspoon monosodium glutamate
2 tablespoons sugar	2–3 red peppers or ¼ teaspoon red
2 tablespoons *mirin*	pepper

Fresh bamboo shoot should be boiled until it is tender; tinned shoots may simply be drained. Slice the bamboo shoot into julienne strips. If red peppers are used, slice into fine rings. Mix together the vinegar, sugar, *mirin*, salt and monosodium glutamate in a small saucepan and heat until the sugar dissolves. Remove from the fire and add the pepper rings or the powdered red pepper. Pour the dressing over the bamboo shoots, let them marinate until cool and serve.

SAUTEED GREEN PEPPERS

12–15 green peppers	3 tablespoons dark soy sauce
2 tablespoons salad oil	1 teaspoon sugar
2 teaspoons sesame oil	Monosodium glutamate

Cut the green peppers into quarters, removing the stems, seeds and
membranes. Heat the oils in a large frying pan. Add the green peppers
and sauté over a hot flame for three or four minutes. Add the soy sauce,
sugar and monosodium glutamate and continue to cook until tender.
Serve immediately.

KIMPIRA (*Braised Burdock Root*)

2 burdock roots	1 tablespoon oil
1 tablespoon dark soy sauce	Salt
1 teaspoon *mirin*	Monosodium glutamate
2 teaspoons sugar	¼ teaspoon red pepper

Peel the burdock root by scraping with the back of a knife. The outer
layer will come off easily. Cut into match-like strips, about 1½ inches
long. Put into cold water to prevent discoloration. Before cooking drain
and dry in a cloth. Heat the oil in a heavy saucepan. Add the sliced burdock root and stir constantly for one minute, keeping the heat high.
Quickly add all the other ingredients and continue stirring over high
heat for two or three minutes longer. Cooking should take no more than
five or six minutes altogether. Remove from the fire and turn out into a
serving bowl. This dish may be eaten either hot or at room temperature.

RENKON KIMPIRA (*Braised Lotus Root*)

1 lotus root

Substitute the lotus root for the burdock roots. Peel the lotus root and
slice into thin rounds, then proceed as in the above recipe.

TAKENOKO KIMPIRA (*Braised Bamboo Shoots*)

2 bamboo shoots (about 8 oz)

Substitute the bamboo shoots for the burdock root. Drain away all
water if tinned shoots are used; if fresh, boil until tender. Slice in rounds
and follow the above recipe.

MUSHROOMS WITH BEAN CURD DRESSING

12 large fresh mushrooms	2 oz white bean paste, *shiro-miso*
½ carrot	Monosodium glutamate
A few *mitsuba* leaves or a small	2 tablespoons white seasame seeds
bunch of parsley	1 teaspoon *mirin*
½lb bean curd, *tōfu*	1 teaspoon sugar

Wash the mushrooms, drain, and cut off the tough stems. Salt lightly and cook under a hot grill for a few minutes, about three or four minutes on each side. Remove and cut into thin slices. Scrape the carrot and cut into thin slices about the same size as the mushrooms. Bring a pan of salted water to the boil, drop in the carrot and cook for one or two minutes, until tender but still crisp. Drain and dry thoroughly. If *mitsuba* leaves are available dip into boiling water, remove immediately and chop finely. If using parsley, chop finely. Parch the sesame seeds in a dry frying pan, stirring constantly, until they begin to jump. Remove and crush in a *suribachi* or mortar, or put through a nut grinder. Add the bean curd to the sesame seeds, then the bean paste, *mirin*, sugar and monosodium glutamate. Add the mushrooms, carrots and *mitsuba*, toss gently with the dressing and serve.

SCALLOP AND SPRING ONION SALAD WITH BEAN PASTE DRESSING

12 scallops	3 tablespoons vinegar
12 spring onions	1 tablespoon sugar
6 tablespoons white bean paste,	2 teaspoons mustard
shiro-miso	

Drop the scallops in boiling salted water and cook until tender, two or three minutes. Drain, cool and cut each scallop into three or four pieces. Clean the spring onions and dip into salted boiling water for about thirty seconds. Remove and drain well, squeezing out the excess water with your hands. Cut into 1½-inch lengths, including the green tops. Mix together the bean paste, vinegar, sugar and mustard. This dressing should be about the same consistency as mayonnaise; if too thick, thin with a little more vinegar. Put the scallops and onions in a bowl, pour the dressing over the top, mix gently and serve.

TUNA AND SPRING ONION SALAD WITH BEAN PASTE DRESSING

½ lb raw tuna

Follow the recipe above but substitute tuna for the scallops. If the tuna is of good quality, and fresh, it is far more delicious raw than cooked and the only preparation necessary is to cut it into ½-inch cubes.

SQUID AND SPRING ONION SALAD WITH BEAN PASTE DRESSING

1 squid

Follow the recipe for scallops and spring onions, but substitute squid for the scallops. Have the fishmonger remove the skin and entrails of the squid, or follow the instructions on page 103. Wash carefully. Boil in salted water for four or five minutes or until the flesh turns white. Remove, drain and cut into pieces 1 inch long and ½ inch wide. Proceed as above.

KINOMEAE (*Bamboo Shoot and Squid Salad with Bean Paste Dressing*)

1 squid
½ lb bamboo shoots
10–12 *kinome* leaves
10–12 spinach leaves
1 cup *dashi* or other stock
2 tablespoons soy sauce

1 tablespoon *mirin*
4 tablespoons white bean paste,
    shiro-miso
2 tablespoons sugar
A little *dashi* broth

Have the fishmonger skin the squid and remove its entrails, or follow the instructions on page 103. Wash well and boil in salted water for five minutes or until the squid turns white. Drain the squid, cool and cut it into bite-size pieces. Wash the bamboo shoot and cut into pieces roughly the same size as those of the squid. Put the *dashi* or stock, soy sauce and *mirin* into a small saucepan and simmer the bamboo shoots in this mixture for ten minutes. Remove and drain.

Wash the *kinome* and spinach leaves and put them in a *suribachi* or into a blender. Add the bean paste, sugar and a little *dashi* broth and blend together until the mixture is a smooth paste. The dressing should be the consistency of mayonnaise. Put the squid and bamboo shoots in a bowl, pour the dressing over the top and mix gently. Garnish with a leaf or two of *kinome* before serving.

GREEN BEAN AND PORK SALAD WITH BEAN CURD DRESSING

¾ lb lean pork
¾ lb green beans
1 piece bean curd, *tōfu* (about 1 lb)
¼ cup white sesame seeds
½ teaspoon salt

2 tablespoons sugar
2 tablespoons light soy sauce
¼ teaspoon monosodium glutamate
1–2 tablespoons *dashi* or other stock

Cut the pork into strips 1½ inches long and ¼ inch wide. Drop into salted boiling water and simmer for three or four minutes or until done. Drain and reserve. String the green beans and boil in salted water for ten minutes or until tender. Drain well and mix with the pork slices. If the beans are very large cut into halves.

Toast the sesame seeds in a dry frying pan. Remove and crush in a *suribachi* or mortar, or put through a nut grinder. Add the crushed seeds to the bean curd along with the sugar, soy sauce, salt and mono-sodium glutamate. If necessary, thin out a little with *dashi* or other stock. This dressing should not be quite so thick as the one in the recipe above. Pour over the pork and beans, mix gently and serve.

CUCUMBER AND FRIED BEAN CURD WITH BEAN CURD DRESSING

1 cucumber
6 oz fried bean curd, *aburage*
3 tablespoons *dashi* or other broth
2 tablespoons soy sauce
1 tablespoon sugar
1 piece bean curd, *tōfu* (about 1 lb)

1 tablespoon sugar
1 tablespoon light soy sauce
2 tablespoons vinegar
2 tablespoons white sesame seeds
Monosodium glutamate

Bring a saucepan of salted water to the boil and put in the cucumber, leaving for about ten seconds. Remove, rinse under cold water and drain. Cut into thin slices, salt lightly and allow to stand for thirty minutes. Spread out the fried bean curd flat and pour boiling water over its surface to wash away any excess oil. Cut the fried bean curd into slices about 1½ inches long and ½ inch wide. Put the *dashi* broth, soy sauce, sugar and a dash of monosodium glutamate into a small saucepan and bring to the boil. Add the fried bean curd slices and simmer until the liquid is absorbed and pieces are well-flavoured.

Wrap the bean curd in a clean cloth and press firmly to remove excess water. Toast the sesame seeds in a dry frying pan and then crush them. Add the crushed sesame seeds to the bean curd along with the sugar, vinegar, soy sauce and a dash of monosodium glutamate. Mix well until the dressing is of a very smooth mayonnaise-like consistency. Place the cucumber slices and fried bean curd into a bowl, cover with the bean curd dressing and mix gently. Allow to stand for about one hour before serving.

HŌRENSŌ-NO-OSHITASHI (Spinach with Soy Sauce Dressing)

1 lb spinach
1 teaspoon salt
2 tablespoons light soy sauce

½ cup *dashi* broth
Dried bonito flakes, *itogatsuo*

Wash the spinach well and do not remove stems unless they are tough. Tie the spinach together so that the stems lie together and the leaves together. Bring a large kettle of salted water to the boil and add the spinach, pushing it under the surface of the water. Let the water come to the boil again and cook for two or three minutes, taking care that it is not cooked too long or its vivid green colour will be lost. Remove from the water and cool rapidly, which will help maintain the brightness of colour. Squeeze out the excess water, either by hand or by rolling the spinach up in a bamboo mat and pressing firmly. Remove the twine. The spinach should now form a neat, bright green cylinder.

Cut the spinach into lengths of 1½ to 2 inches and carefully put each length onto a small individual plate. Mix together the soy sauce and *dashi* broth and pour over the spinach. Garnish with a sprinkling of dried bonito flakes if possible.

SPINACH WITH SESAME SEEDS

1 lb fresh spinach	1 tablespoon sugar
3 tablespoons white sesame seeds	Monosodium glutamate
3 tablespoons light soy sauce	

Wash the spinach carefully and cook as in the above recipe. Rinse in cold water and drain well. Cut the spinach in ¾-inch lengths and mix with one and a half tablespoons soy sauce.

Heat the sesame seeds in a dry, heavy frying pan until they begin to jump. Stir constantly so that they don't burn. Remove from the fire and crush the seeds in a mortar or *suribachi*, or put them through a nut grinder. Mix the sesame seeds with the remaining soy sauce, the sugar and monosodium glutamate. Pour the sesame seed sauce over the spinach. Serve at room temperature, arranged on individual salad plates.

SPINACH WITH CRUSHED PEANUTS

1 lb fresh spinach	2½ tablespoons soy sauce
½ cup peanuts	Monosodium glutamate

Wash the spinach carefully and cook as described above. Rinse in cold water and drain well. Cut the spinach into ¾-inch lengths and mix with one and a half tablespoons soy sauce. Heat the peanuts in a dry frying pan for five or ten minutes, taking care not to let them burn. Remove from the fire and grind to a paste in a mortar or *suribachi*, or in a blender. Add one tablespoon soy sauce and a dash of monosodium glutamate, and mix well. Mix this sauce with the spinach and serve.

MATSUTAKE TSUTSUMI-YAKI

The arrival in early October of the *matsutake* mushrooms, fatly nestling in their beds of fern, is one of the first signs that autumn is truly here. The first arrivals of the season command an enormous price, which gradually descends as the short season advances to a level only moderately exorbitant. They are, however, superb, with an aroma and flavour and a certain crispness of texture quite unlike any other mushroom. The *matsutake*, or pine mushroom, takes its name from the red pine forests in which it is found. Its size varies enormously from the small young mushrooms about the size of an egg to the enormous ones as much as 8 to 10 inches across.

12 *matsutake* mushrooms (or champignons)	2 tablespoons *mirin*
	2 tablespoons lemon juice
4 teaspoons soy sauce	½ teaspoon monosodium glutamate

Wash the mushroom thoroughly in a solution of salt water. Cut away any hard parts of the stems, but do not remove the skin. Enclose the mushrooms in aluminium foil and seal the packages tightly. Cook under a hot grill, turning the packages over frequently, until the mushrooms are soft to the touch. Remove from the foil. Mix together the soy sauce, lemon juice, *mirin* and monosodium glutamate, pour over the hot mushrooms and serve immediately.

STUFFED MUSHROOMS

20 dried mushrooms	½ egg white
1 cup *dashi* or chicken stock	1 teaspoon salt
2 tablespoons soy sauce	Monosodium glutamate
2 tablespoons *mirin* or sugar	1 teaspoon cornflour
½ lb shelled shrimps	

Cover the dried mushrooms with cold water and soak until soft, about fifteen minutes. Remove the stems. Put the broth, soy sauce and *mirin* or sugar into a saucepan and bring to the boil. Add the mushrooms and simmer for ten minutes or until the mushrooms have absorbed most of the liquid. Remove from the fire and drain. Make a past of the shrimps (they should be cleaned and shelled and tinned or frozen ones are quite suitable) by putting them in a *suribachi*, mortar or blender and mixing until they assume a paste-like consistency. Add the egg white, cornflour, salt and a dash of monosodium glutamate and continue to mix until the paste is smooth. Add more egg white if necessary. Put a spoonful of the shrimp paste on the underside of the each mushroom, spreading it until it fills the cavity. Steam the mushrooms until the shrimp paste is set. They may be eaten hot or at room temperature.

YAKI MATSUTAKE (*Grilled Mushrooms*)

4 large *matsutake* mushrooms or   4 tablespoons soy sauce
  12 large fresh mushrooms of   1 lemon
  another variety   Monosodium glutamate

Carefully wash the mushrooms, trimming away any hard parts on the
stem. If the mushrooms are to stand for any time before cooking, put
into cold water with a little salt dissolved in it. Heat the grill and drain
and dry the mushrooms. Put the mushrooms under the grill and cook
until they become barely tender. Do not overcook or they will be dry
and tasteless. Remove to a serving plate, letting each person sprinkle on
soy sauce, lemon juice and monosodium glutamate to taste.

MUSHROOMS GRILLED WITH MIRIN

6 *matsutake* mushrooms or other   ¼ cup *mirin*
  large, fresh mushrooms   1½ tablespoons light soy sauce

Mix together the *mirin* and soy sauce. Wash the mushrooms and slice
into three or four pieces each. Marinate for one hour in the soy sauce
and *mirin* mixture. Remove, drain well and cook under a hot grill for
two or three minutes on each side. Brush once or twice with the marinade while cooking. When tender remove, arrange on a plate and serve
immediately.

SAUTEED MUSHROOMS AND CUCUMBERS

1 cucumber   2 tablespoons oil
Salt   3 tablespoons soy sauce
6 large fresh mushrooms   2 teaspoons sugar
2 tablespoons sesame seeds   ¼ teaspoon monosodium glutamate

Wash the cucumber, cut into rounds, and sprinkle with salt. Allow to
stand for thirty minutes. Wash the mushrooms carefully and cut into
slices about ¼ inch wide. Toast the sesame seeds in a dry frying pan,

stirring slowly, until they begin to jump. Remove, crush in a *suribachi* or mortar, or put through a nut grinder. Put the oil into the frying pan and heat. Dry the cucumber slices and add both the cucumbers and mushrooms to the hot oil, sautéeing over a hot fire until the cucumbers become pliable. Add the sugar and soy sauce and cook for a further minute or two. Remove to a serving dish, sprinkle with sesame seeds and serve immediately.

DOBIN MUSHI (*Mushrooms in a Teapot*)

This dish is a favourite when *matsutake* mushrooms are in season. It is essentially a soup, but is given greater piquancy by being prepared in and served from an earthenware teapot, accompanied by teabowls from which the broth is drunk and into which the morsels of mushroom, shrimp and chicken are placed.

3 *matsutake* mushrooms or 6 large firm mushrooms of another variety	1 lemon
	4 cups *dashi*
	½ teaspoon salt
1 chicken breast	1 tablespoon light soy sauce
6 prawns	¼ teaspoon monosodium glutamate
3 oz chrysanthemum leaves	

Clean and wash the mushrooms, trimming away the tough parts of the stem, and slice. Remove the bone and skin from the breast of chicken and cut the meat into bite-size pieces. Remove the heads and shells of the prawns, leaving the tail intact. Wash thoroughly and de-vein. Wash the chrysanthemum leaves and chop roughly. Put the *dashi* into a saucepan, add the salt, monosodium glutamate, and soy sauce and bring to the boil. Taste for seasoning and correct if necessary. It is important in this dish that the colour of the broth should not be impaired, so salt is preferred to soy sauce for seasoning.

Put the mushrooms, chicken and prawns in the teapot and pour the boiling broth over the top. Put on the lid and cook over a gentle heat for fifteen to twenty minutes, skimming the top occasionally. Add the chrysanthemum leaves, cook for thirty seconds longer and remove from the fire. Add the juice of one lemon and serve.

EGGPLANT WITH MUSTARD DRESSING

Japanese eggplants are much smaller than the European variety, three Japanese ones being equal to about one European eggplant in weight. The amounts called for here are for the European size.

1 eggplant	2 tablespoons soy sauce
1½ tablespoons vinegar	1½ tablespoons vinegar
1 teaspoon salt	¼ teaspoon monosodium glutamate
2 teaspoons mustard	

Wash the eggplant and without peeling cut into ¼-inch slices. Sprinkle with salt and leave for thirty minutes. Drain off the liquid and pat dry with a clean cloth. Sprinkle over the vinegar, toss gently and dry again. Mix the mustard to a smooth paste with a little water, then combine with the soy sauce, vinegar and monosodium glutamate. Pour over the eggplant slices, toss gently and serve immediately.

EGGPLANT STUFFED WITH PORK

3 small eggplants	2 teaspoons soy sauce
¾ lb minced pork	2 tablespoons *sake*
1 egg	¼ teaspoon pepper
2 spring onions	¼ teaspoon monosodium glutamate
2-inch piece of fresh ginger root	2 tablespoons cornflour
2 tablespoons white sesame seeds	A pint or more of vegetable oil

Cut the eggplants into halves and scoop out the centre. Submerge the eggplants in cold water to prevent their turning brown. Prepare the stuffing. Chop the spring onions finely and grate the ginger. Mix together in a bowl the pork, chopped onions, grated ginger and its juice, and the egg. Add the seasonings of pepper, soy sauce, *sake* and monosodium glutamate and mix again. Drain the eggplants and dry thoroughly. Coat their inside surfaces with cornflour. Stuff with the pork mixture, pressing down firmly. Sprinkle with the sesame seeds which have been toasted in a dry frying pan. Heat the oil in a deep pan and add the eggplants, frying until they and the pork stuffing are done. Since they are large and the pork must be thoroughly cooked this will take longer than most deep fat frying and hence the temperature of the oil should be slightly lower to avoid burning the outside surface. Remove, drain for a moment or two and serve immediately.

MUSHINASU (*Steamed Eggplant*)

2 eggplants	2 tablespoons black sesame seeds
Salt	2 tablespoons soy sauce
¼ cup dried bonito flakes,	½ teaspoon monosodium glutamate
itogatsuo (optional)	

Peel the eggplant and submerge in cold water to prevent discoloration. Cut into thick slices, sprinkle with salt and steam until tender. While the eggplant is steaming, parch the sesame seeds in a dry frying pan until they begin to jump. Remove the eggplant slices to a serving plate, sprinkle with the sesame seeds, and soy sauce and monosodium glutamate to taste. Add a sprinkling of dried bonito flakes if available and serve.

GRILLED EGGPLANTS WITH CHICKEN SAUCE

2 eggplants	1 tablespoon sugar
2 tablespoons salad oil	4 tablespoons red bean paste,
Salt	*aka-miso*
Monosodium glutamate	¾ cup chicken stock
½ lb minced chicken	½ teaspoon salt
1½ tablespoons *sake*	

Split the eggplants in half or, if very large, into slices about 1 inch thick. Do not peel. Brush them with oil and sprinkle lightly with salt and monosodium glutamate and grill until soft. In the meantime heat the remaining oil in a frying pan and add the chicken, frying for a minute or two. Add the *sake*, sugar, bean paste, stock and salt and simmer for ten minutes. Arrange the grilled eggplants on a platter, pour the chicken sauce over the top and serve immediately.

GRILLED EGGPLANT WITH SESAME SEEDS

2 eggplants	2 tablespoons dark soy sauce
2 tablespoons white sesame seeds	1 teaspoon sugar
4 spring onions	¼ teaspoon monosodium glutamate
¼ teaspoon red pepper	

Cut the eggplants into slices about 1 inch thick. Do not peel. Salt and allow to stand for thirty minutes. Drain away excess water and pat dry with a clean cloth. Sprinkle lightly with salt again and grill until soft. In the meantime toast the sesame seeds in a dry frying pan until they start jumping. Remove and crush in a *suribachi* or mortar, or put through a nut grinder. Clean the spring onions and chop finely, using most of the green tops as well. Combine the sesame seeds, green onions, red pepper, soy sauce, sugar and monosodium glutamate in a small saucepan and heat until warm. Arrange the grilled eggplant slices on a platter, spread the sesame seed mixture over the top and serve immediately.

EGGPLANT DRESSED WITH GINGER

1 eggplant	1 tablespoon *sake*
Salt	1 teaspoon sugar
2-inch piece of fresh ginger root	¼ teaspoon monosodium glutamate
½ cup light soy sauce	

Wash the eggplant. Without peeling, cut it into strips about 1½ inches long and ¼ inch wide. Sprinkle with salt and allow to stand for thirty minutes. Drain away the water and pat dry with a clean cloth. Combine the soy sauce, *sake*, sugar and monosodium glutamate. Peel the ginger and cut it into extremely fine shreds. Add the ginger and eggplant to the soy mixture and marinate two hours before serving.

NASU SHIGIYAKI (Grilled Eggplant with Bean Paste)

2 eggplants	2 tablespoons *mirin*
2 tablespoons vegetable oil	2 tablespoons *dashi* or other stock
4 tablespoons red bean paste, *miso*	Monosodium glutamate
2 tablespoons sugar	

Cut the eggplants into round slices about ½ inch thick. Japanese eggplants are much smaller than the European variety and normally the entire round is used, but if you use exceptionally large eggplants it may be more convenient to cut these rounds into halves. Brush the slices with

oil and grill on both sides until the eggplant becomes soft. In the meantime mix together the bean paste, sugar, *mirin*, stock and a dash of
monosodium glutamate. Remove from the grill and brush with the bean
paste mixture. Return to the grill and cook under a low flame until the
paste is dry and has formed a glaze. This operation requires some care
since bean paste burns easily. Remove and serve immediately.

NEGI SHIGIYAKI (*Grilled Leeks with Bean Paste*)

6 leeks

Clean the leeks and cut into 1½-inch lengths. Put three or four on a
skewer, brush with oil and proceed as in the above recipe.

GRILLED LEEKS

12 leeks   4 tablespoons dark soy sauce
1 tablespoon sesame seed oil   ¼ teaspoon monosodium glutamate
¼ teaspoon red pepper

Wash the leeks thoroughly and cut the white part into pieces 1½ inches
long. Brush with sesame seed oil and grill them under a medium flame
in a pre-heated grill until they begin to turn brown. Mix together the
red pepper, soy sauce and monosodium glutamate. Remove the leeks
from the grill and brush with the soy sauce mixture. Return to the grill
and cook until they are tender. Remove to a serving dish and pour over
them any liquid which has accumulated in the bottom of the pan. Serve
immediately.

LEEKS WRAPPED IN PORK

12 leeks   ½ cup soy sauce
1¼ lb lean pork   1 tablespoon sugar
2 tablespoons oil   4 tablespoons *sake*

Wash the leeks thoroughly and cut away the green stalks. If they are very long cut them into approximately 4-inch lengths. Have the pork sliced very thin, no thicker than bacon. Wrap each leek in a slice of pork and secure with a toothpick or two. Heat the oil in a frying pan and add the leeks, frying and turning until they are browned on all sides. Add the soy sauce, sugar and *sake*, lower the flame and cover. Simmer for three or four minutes, until the leeks are tender. Remove the lid and shake the frying pan vigorously, turning the leeks so that they become coated with the sauce. Remove to a serving dish and remove the toothpicks. Pour over them the remaining sauce and serve. These may be kept warm in the oven with little damage to their flavour for twenty to thirty minutes before serving.

YAKI TAKENOKO (Grilled Bamboo Shoots)

2 bamboo shoots
¼ cup dried bonito flakes, *katsuo* (optional)
½ cup soy sauce
¼ cup *sake*

Drain the bamboo shoots and cut into slices about ⅓ inch thick. Put the soy sauce, *sake* and, if available, dried bonito flakes into a small saucepan, bring to the boil and remove immediately. If bonito flakes have been used strain the sauce. Marinate the bamboo shoots in this mixture for fifteen minutes. Heat the grill and cook the bamboo shoots under it. Use a fairly low flame and grill for seven or eight minutes on each side. Brush three or four times with the marinade while cooking. Remove and serve immediately.

KINOME NO TAKENOKO YAKI (Sauteed Bamboo Shoots)

2 bamboo shoots
1 tablespoon oil
15–20 *kinome* leaves or 1 small bunch of parsley
¼ cup soy sauce
2 tablespoons *mirin*
1 tablespoon *sake*

Drain the bamboo shoots and cut into rounds about ⅓ inch thick. Chop finely a little more than half of the *kinome* leaves or parsley. Mix together with the soy sauce, *mirin* and *sake*. Heat a little oil in a frying pan, add the bamboo shoots and fry over a hot flame until they begin to turn brown, tossing and turning continually with a spatula or chopsticks. Pour in the soy sauce mixture and continue to fry for a further four or five minutes. Put in a serving dish, garnish with the remaining *kinome* leaves or parsley and serve immediately.

CABBAGE ROLLS

12 large cabbage leaves	½ teaspoon salt
6 pieces of fried bean curd, *aburage*	1 teaspoon sugar
1 lb minced pork	2½ cups *dashi* or chicken stock
4 large dried mushrooms	1 tablespoon soy sauce
3 spring onions	½ teaspoon salt
1 egg	1 teaspoon sugar
1 tablespoon *sake*	¼ teaspoon monosodium glutamate

Separate the cabbage leaves carefully from the head and dip them in and out of boiling water, leaving them just long enough to become pliable. Drain well. Cut along three sides of the pieces of fried bean curd, opening them into flat sheets. Put in a colander and pour boiling water over them to remove any excess oil. Drain well. Soak the dried mushrooms in cold water until soft, drain and mince. Mince the spring onions and add to the pork along with the minced mushrooms, *sake*, salt, sugar and egg. Mix well.

Spread out the cabbage leaves in pairs, the sides overlapping. Spread a little of the pork mixture over them. Place a sheet of fried bean curd on top of the pork and then spread the remaining pork mixture on top of the bean curd. Roll the cabbage leaves up, tucking in the ends and securing the rolls by tying with twine.

In a large bottomed saucepan heat the stock, one tablespoon of soy sauce, half teaspoon salt, one teaspoon sugar and the monosodium glutamate. Add the cabbage rolls, cover with a lid and simmer until the meat is done and the cabbage well-flavoured, twenty or thirty minutes. Turn the rolls occasionally during the cooking. Remove the cabbage rolls to a serving platter, take off the twine and pour the sauce over the top.

ROLLED CHINESE CABBAGE AND SPINACH

The two shades of green makes this an attractive dish, and cabbage and spinach prepared in this way is often used in casserole dishes instead of plain, raw cabbage.

1 small head of Chinese cabbage   8 oz fresh spinach

Boil the spinach briefly, keeping it in a neat cylinder as described in the recipe for spinach with soy sauce dressing on page 141. Separate the leaves of the Chinese cabbage and dip into boiling salted water until just tender. Remove and drain carefully. Spread out two or three leaves of the cabbage in a neat square, arrange a few strands of the spinach across the cabbage in a neat line. Roll the cabbage from the bottom into a tight roll and squeeze out any excess water. Leave for fifteen or twenty minutes in the rolled position and then cut into 1½-inch lengths.

CHINESE CABBAGE AND SCALLOPS

½ head of Chinese cabbage   1-inch piece of fresh ginger root
¾ lb scallops   2 tablespoons soy sauce
1 small carrot   ½ teaspoon salt
1 small bamboo shoot   1 tablespoon cornflour
2 tablespoons oil   Monosodium glutamate
1 cup chicken stock   ¼ teaspoon pepper

Cut the Chinese cabbage into large pieces, about 3 inches in length and 2 inches wide. Scrape the carrot and cut it into strips about 3 inches long and ⅛ inch thick. Drain the bamboo shoot and cut into pieces about ¼ inch thick. Wash the scallops and score them across the top in a checkerboard pattern. Heat the oil in a frying pan and when it becomes hot add the scallops, carrots and bamboo shoots and fry for three or four minutes, maintaining a high heat and tossing the vegetables and fish constantly to prevent burning. Then add the Chinese cabbage. Fry for another minute, then add the chicken stock. When it begins to boil add the soy sauce, the ginger after it has been grated, pepper and a dash of monosodium glutamate. Mix the cornflour into a little cold water, add to the stock and bring to the boil again. When the stock has thickened slightly remove, put the vegetables and scallops on a serving plate, pour the sauce over them and serve immediately.

STEAMED CHINESE CABBAGE AND PORK

15–16 leaves of Chinese cabbage
¾ lb lean pork
3 tablespoons soy sauce
2 teaspoons sugar
1-inch piece of fresh ginger root
⅓ cup *sake*

½ teaspoon salt
1 cup stock
¼ teaspoon monosodium glutamate
¼ teaspoon red pepper
1 tablespoon cornflour

Carefully separate the leaves from the head of cabbage. Bring a saucepan of water to the boil and add the leaves, taking care that they aren't broken. Remove after thirty seconds, drain well and sprinkle with salt. Have the pork cut very thin, no thicker than bacon. Marinate it for twenty minutes in a mixture of the soy sauce, sugar and ginger juice, derived from grating the ginger and squeezing the juice out by hand. Cut the cabbage leaves into halves. Make six mounds of alternating layers of the cabbage and pork, starting and ending with the cabbage leaves. Put into a steamer and sprinkle with the red pepper or, better, with a few rings sliced from whole red peppers. Sprinkle the *sake* and salt over the top and steam for fifteen to twenty minutes. Remove the cabbage mounds to a serving platter and keep warm. Drain off any juice which accumulated during the steaming and add it to the chicken stock in a separate saucepan. Bring to the boil, add any marinade which remains, the monosodium glutamate and the green peas. Cook for five minutes and thicken with the cornflour dissolved in cold water. Pour the sauce over the cabbage mounds and serve immediately.

TAKIAWASE (*Bamboo Shoots and Chicken Dumplings*)

INGREDIENTS FOR DUMPLINGS

¾ lb minced chicken
¾ cup fine dry bread crumbs
1 egg
1½ tablespoons white bean paste,
  shiro-miso

3 tablespoons *dashi* or chicken
  stock
¾ tablespoon soy sauce
½ teaspoon salt
¼ teaspoon monosodium glutamate

To make dumplings: Put the minced chicken into a *suribachi* or into an ordinary bowl and add the bread crumbs, egg and bean paste and mix well. Add the *dashi*, soy sauce, salt and monsodium glutamate and mix again. Form the chicken mixture into small balls. Cook by dropping into boiling water and simmering gently for five to seven minutes. Remove and drain.

OTHER INGREDIENTS

2–4 bamboo shoots	1 tablespoon sugar
6–12 large mushrooms	1 teaspoon salt
3 cups *dashi* or chicken stock	A few *sansho* leaves, watercress,
3 tablespoons light soy sauce	or parsley
2 tablespoons *mirin*	

Drain the bamboo shoots and cut off about 1½ inches of the tips, then cut the tips into halves. Cut the remainder of the bamboo shoots into ½-inch thick rounds. Put the bamboo shoots, mushrooms and chicken dumplings into a large saucepan and add the *dashi*, soy sauce, *mirin*, salt and sugar. Simmer over a low fire for twenty to twenty-five minutes. Remove from the fire and allow to stand in the liquid for a few minutes. Drain and arrange the vegetables in a serving bowl. Garnish with a few sprigs of fresh *sansho* leaves, watercress, or parsley.

SUEHIRO TAKENOKO (*Boiled Bamboo Shoots*)

3 tinned bamboo shoots	1–2 teaspoons soy sauce
2 cups *dashi* broth	¼ teaspoon monosodium glutamate
1 tablespoon sugar	

Cut the bamboo shoots in half and then into strips about ½ inch thick. Combine the remaining ingredients in a saucepan, bring to the boil, add the bamboo shoots and simmer for fifteen minutes Remove and drain.

SAUTEED BROAD BEANS

3 cups shelled fresh broad beans	1 tablespoon sugar
2 tablespoons oil	2 tablespoons *sake*
4 tablespoons soy sauce	¼ teaspoon monosodium glutamate

Shell the beans. Heat the oil in a frying pan and when hot add the beans. Keep the fire high, and fry until they begin to brown, turning and tossing the beans constantly with a spatula. Add the soy sauce, sugar, *sake*, and monosodium glutamate. Continue to cook until the beans are tender, turn out into a bowl and serve immediately.

KURI KINTON (*Mashed Sweet Potato with Chestnuts*)

¾ lb sweet potatoes   10–12 tinned sweetened chestnuts
½ cup sugar   1 tablespoon burnt alum
3 tablespoons *mirin*   (optional)

Peel the potatoes and cut into 1-inch cubes. If burnt alum is used in order to preserve the colour, the potatoes should be soaked for four to five hours in water in which the alum has been dissolved. Before cooking, drain and rinse thoroughly. Cook the potatoes in boiling water until tender and drain. Mash the potatoes while still hot and mix in half of the sugar, beating until smooth. Put the *mirin* in a small saucepan and reduce it to half its volume. Add the sugar and cook until it dissolves. Add the mashed sweet potatoes to the *mirin* and sugar mixture and cook slowly over a low flame, stirring constantly, until the mixture is about the same consistency as jam. Cut the chestnuts into quarters and mix into the potatoes. Serve at room temperature.

RINGO KINTON (*Mashed Sweet Potato with Apples*)

Ingredients as above, plus 2 apples

Prepare the sweet potatoes as described above and shortly before serving mix in two sliced apples.

MATCHA KINTON (*Mashed Sweet Potato with Green Tea*)

Ingredients as above plus 2 tablespoons powdered green tea, *matcha*

Prepare the sweet potatoes as described above. Dissolve the green tea powder in a little boiling water and mix it into the cooled sweet potato mixture.

FUROFUKI DAIKON (*Turnips Stuffed with Bean Paste*) .

The dishes of Kyoto, the ancient capital of Japan, are known for their plain, refined flavours, seasoning being used sparingly in an attempt to enhance the natural taste of ingredients. By Japanese standards Kyoto lies far from the sea and its geographical position combined with its status as the centre of Japanese Buddhism make it not unnatural that the cooks of Kyoto have for centuries concentrated on vegetables rather than fish or meats.

6 small turnips	2 cups white or red bean paste,
1 teaspoon salt	*miso*
3 cups *dashi* broth	2 tablespoons sugar
1 6-inch piece of *kombu* seaweed,	4 tablespoons *sake*
kelp	2 tablespoons *mirin*
2 tablespoons light soy sauce	3 tablespoons *dashi* broth
½ teaspoon salt	1 egg yolk
¼ teaspoon monosodium glutamate	1 lemon rind

Wash the turnips and leave whole. Trim the leaves off the top, but leave about ½ inch of the stem Drop the turnips into boiling salted water and parboil for eight minutes. Remove the turnips, rinse under cold water and drain in a colander.

Put a piece of *kombu* seaweed in a saucepan and cover with the *dashi* broth. Bring to the boil and remove the seaweed. (If *kombu* seaweed is not available it can be omitted without drastically changing the taste of the turnips.) Add the sugar, soy sauce, salt and monosodium glutamate. Drop in the turnips, bring the liquid to the boil and cook the turnips until they are tender. Set aside and keep warm.

Put the bean paste, two tablespoons sugar, four tablespoons *sake*, two tablespoons *mirin*, the egg yolk and grated lemon rind in a bowl and mix thoroughly, until light and smooth. Put this bean paste mixture into the top of a double boiler and cook for five to ten minutes, until the mixture thickens slightly. Drain the turnips and cut off the tops. Scoop out a neat hole in the centre of each, fill with the bean paste mixture, replace the tops and serve. Alternatively, you can simply pour the sauce over the tops of the turnips.

SQUASH (OR MARROW) WITH BEAN PASTE SAUCE

1½ lb squash or marrow

Substitute squash or marrow for the turnips in the above recipe. Cut it into large pieces and cook in the *dashi* broth without parboiling. Then proceed as in the above recipe. To serve, pour the *miso* sauce over the top of the squash or marrow slices.

The Japanese squash is about the size of a large grapefruit, similar in flavour and texture to the American acorn squash. The English marrow will do.

BOILED SQUASH (OR MARROW)

1½ lb squash or marrow	1 teaspoon salt
3 cups *dashi* or chicken stock	3 tablespoons light soy sauce
2 tablespoons sugar	¼ teaspoon monosodium glutamate

Peel the squash or marrow and cut into chunks about 1½ inches square. Bring the soup stock and other seasonings to the boil, and add the vegetable. Bring to a gentle boil again and cook for ten to fifteen minutes or until the squash or marrow is tender. Drain and serve while hot. (*See* above for note on Japanese squash.)

STEWED PORK AND SQUASH (OR MARROW)

1½ lb squash or marrow	1 teaspoon salt
½ lb lean pork	½ teaspoon pepper
2 cups *dashi* or chicken stock	Monosodium glutamate
2 tablespoons oil	1 tablespoon light soy sauce

Cut the pork into cubes about 1 inch square. Peel the squash or marrow and cut it into cubes of a slightly larger size. Put a little of the oil into a frying pan and heat. Add the pork and brown quickly. Remove, add more oil if necessary and fry the squash or marrow until slightly brown. Drain away any excess oil and put the pork back into the frying pan with the vegetable. Add salt, pepper and monosodium glutamate and

pour on the *dashi*. Bring to the boil and reduce heat. Add the soy sauce
and continue to simmer until the squash or marrow is tender and the
liquid almost absorbed. Taste for seasoning, correct if necessary and
serve immediately. (*See* above for note on Japanese squash.)

BOILED CARROTS

2 carrots	1 tablespoon sugar
2 cups *dashi* or chicken stock	1–2 teaspoons soy sauce
½ teaspoon salt	¼ teaspoon monosodium glutamate

Scrape the carrots and cut into sections 1 inch thick. These lengths of
carrots are then usually cut into simple flower shapes with an aluminium
cutter. Combine the remaining ingredients in a saucepan, bring to the
boil, add the carrots and cook until tender. Remove and drain.

ODEN

One of the most familiar winter sights in Tokyo or Osaka are the tiny
wooden stalls on wheels serving out their steaming bowls of *oden*.

1 lb grilled bean curd, *yakidōfu*	6 hard-boiled eggs
1 lb *konnyaku*	1½ quarts *dashi* or chicken stock
½ lb Japanese radish, *daikon*	1 tablespoon sugar
3 pieces of fried bean curd, *aburage*	2 tablespoons soy sauce
6 leaves of cabbage	2 teaspoons salt
1 fish sausage, *kamaboko*	2 tablespoons *mirin*
1 carrot	1 teaspoon monosodium glutamate
1 squid	Mustard

Cut the *konnyaku* into triangles of fairly large size. Cut the radish into
chunks. Cut the grilled bean curd into large cubes. Pour boiling water
over the *aburage*, drain and cut into pieces about 2 inches square. Wash
the cabbage leaves and cut roughly. Slice the fish sausage into pieces
about 1 inch thick. Peel the carrot and cut into large pieces. Prepare the
squid as on page 103 and cut it into squares. Put the stock, sugar, soy
sauce, salt and *mirin* into a large saucepan and add the carrot, radish
and fish sausage. Cook for fifteen minutes or until almost tender and
then add the other ingredients. Simmer slowly for twenty minutes. Eat
hot with a little mustard.

BOILED PUMPKIN

1½ lb pumpkin
3 cups *dashi* broth
2 tablespoons sugar

1 tablespoon light soy sauce
1 teaspoon salt

Peel the pumpkin, unless it is very young and tender in which case the skin can be left on. Cut into large pieces. Pour the *dashi* into a saucepan, add the pumpkin and bring to the boil. Reduce to a medium flame and cook until the *dashi* has reduced about one-third. Add the sugar, soy sauce and salt and continue to cook until the pumpkin is tender. Serve hot.

VEGETABLES BOILED WITH CHICKEN

3 potatoes
2 small carrots
2 lotus roots, *renkon*
1 burdock root
1 square *konnyaku* (½ lb)
2 bamboo shoots
1 lb chicken

1 cup *sake*
⅓ cup *mirin*
3 cups *dashi* or chicken stock
5 tablespoons light soy sauce
2 tablespoons sugar
½ cup green peas

Peel the potatoes and cut them into large chunks. Scrape the carrots and cut into fairly large pieces. Peel the lotus roots and slice into rings. Scrape the burdock root with the back of a knife and cut into large pieces. Rinse the *konnyaku* under cold water and tear it into pieces about the same size as the burdock root. If using fresh bamboo shoots, boil until tender; if using tinned, drain well. Cut into slices ½ inch thick. Leave the chicken on the bone and with a heavy meat cleaver chop it into 2-inch lengths.

Pour the *sake* and *mirin* into a large saucepan and heat until warm. Light the mixture with a match, burning off all the alcohol. When the flames have died down add the *dashi* or chicken stock and all the vegetables. Bring quickly to the boil, cook for five minutes and then add the chicken. Cover with a lid and allow the chicken to simmer for about ten minutes. Skim the surface carefully. Add the sugar and soy sauce, re-cover and continue to cook for ten or fifteen minutes, until the chicken is done and the vegetables are tender. Remove from the fire and let stand for ten minutes in a warm place before serving. The vegetables and chicken may either be served with the broth, or drained and served separately.

CHIKUZENNI

1 lb chicken	2 small bamboo shoots
2 small carrots	2 tablespoons oil
1 burdock root	1½ cups *dashi* or chicken stock
1 square *konnyaku* (½ lb)	2 tablespoons sugar
3 potatoes	½ cup light soy sauce

Prepare the chicken and vegetables as in the recipe above. Heat the oil in the bottom of a heavy saucepan and when hot add the vegetables and chicken and fry for a few minutes. When they have begun to brown add the *dashi* or chicken stock, sugar and soy sauce. Cook over a medium flame until most of the liquid has been absorbed and the vegetables are tender. Arrange in a serving dish, pouring any remaining liquid over the top.

EGG DISHES

CHAWAN MUSHI

6 cups *dashi* or chicken broth
1½ cups eggs
2 chicken breasts
1 tablespoon light soy sauce
6 prawns
1 tablespoon *sake*
Salt

6 large fresh mushrooms
1 lemon
1 small bunch *mitsuba* or spinach
   or watercress
1 lily root, *yurine* (optional)
6 slices fish sausage, *kamaboko*
   (optional)

This dish is basically a custard containing pieces of chicken, vegetables, etc, which should be prepared first. Remove the skin, bone and tendon from the chicken breast and cut the meat into slices about 1 inch long and ⅓ inch thick. Sprinkle the chicken with a little soy sauce and leave to marinate. Clean the prawns, removing the head, shell and tail and de-veining them. Cut lengthwise along the inner side of the prawns, not quite cutting through, and open them out flat. Sprinkle with a little *sake* and salt and leave to marinate. Cut six lengths of lemon peel about

1 inch long and $\frac{1}{4}$ inch wide. Clean the mushrooms, cutting away any hard parts of the stem. Cut in halves if very large. Wash the greens and chop roughly into lengths about $1\frac{1}{2}$ inches long. If lily root is available, separate it into segments and boil in a little salted water for four or five minutes. Remove and drain. Pour boiling water over the *kamaboko* and cut it into six slices, each about $\frac{1}{3}$ inch thick.

Heat the broth and taste for seasoning, making sure that it is well-flavoured. Slightly beat the eggs and pour the hot broth over them in a thin stream, mixing well. Do not beat too violently. The surface of the custard mixture should be free from bubbles. Strain and reserve. Drain the chicken and shrimps and arrange them, the mushrooms, lemon peel, lily root and fish sausage in the bottom of six individual casseroles (or one large casserole if preferred). Pour the custard carefully over the top. Place the casseroles in a baking tin and pour boiling water in the tin until it comes about halfway up the sides of the casseroles. Bake in a moderate oven for fifteen minutes. Remove and add the *mitsuba*, spinach, or watercress until it comes about halfway up the sides of the casseroles. Bake in a moderate oven for fifteen minutes. Remove and add the *mitsuba*, spinach, or watercress, pressing it down into the custard. Return the casseroles to the oven and continue to bake until set. Do not bake too long: the surface should be pure yellow, not browned. The custard, though completely set, will always retain some liquid which has drained from the vegetables and fish during the cooking. Since the Japanese regard *chawan mushi* primarily as a soup, there is no objection to this. In fact, *chawan mushi* occupies a rather special place in the Japanese cuisine, it being the only dish which is eaten with a spoon. It is usually served hot, but is occasionally eaten cold in the summer.

ODAMAKI MUSHI (*Steamed Egg Custard with Noodles*)

Ingredients as above plus $\frac{1}{2}$ lb cooked *udon* noodles

This is simply a variation on the dish above in which a layer of cooked noodles is placed on the bottom of the casseroles, the other ingredients are arranged on top of the noodles and the custard poured over to cover them all. *Udon* noodles are usually used in this dish, but an acceptable substitute would be either macaroni or spaghetti.

ANAGO MUSHI (*Steamed Egg Custard with Eel*)

6 cups *dashi* or chicken broth	1 small bunch *mitsuba*, fresh
1½ cups eggs	spinach, or watercress
6 pieces *kabayaki anago*, grilled eel	6 slices fish sausage, *kamaboko*
6 large fresh mushrooms	1 lily root, *yurine* (optional)
1 lemon	

Cook the eel as described on page 100. Clean the mushrooms, trimming away any hard parts of the stems, and slice into halves. Wash the greens and cut into 1½-inch lengths. If lily root is available, separate it into segments and boil in a little salted water for four or five minutes. Remove, drain and reserve. Pour boiling water over the *kamaboko* and cut into six slices, each about ⅓ inch thick. Cut six lengths of lemon peel, each about 1½ inches long and ¼ inch wide.

Heat the broth and taste for seasoning, making sure that it is well-flavoured. Slightly beat the eggs and add the hot broth, a little at a time, mixing well. Strain and reserve. Arrange the eel, mushrooms, *kamaboko*, lily root and lemon peel on the bottom of six individual casseroles or one large casserole. Pour the custard carefully over the top. Place the casseroles in a baking tin and pour boiling water into the tin until it comes about halfway up the sides of the casseroles. Bake in a moderate oven for fifteen minutes. Remove and add the lengths of greens, pushing them down into the custard. Return to the oven and continue to bake until set. Serve hot or cold.

KŌYA MUSHI (*Steamed Egg Custard with Bean Curd*)

1 square bean curd, *tōfu* (about 1 lb)	1 small bunch fresh spinach, *mitsuba*, or watercress
12 scallops	6 cups *dashi* or chicken stock
Salt	1½ cups eggs
6 large fresh mushrooms	1 lily root, *yurine* (optional)

Wrap the bean curd in a clean cloth and press gently to remove the excess water. Cut the bean curd into 2-inch squares and arrange in the bottoms of six individual casseroles. Wash the scallops carefully and dry. Season with a little salt and, if desired, a sprinkling of *sake*. Wash the mushrooms and trim away the hard parts of the stems. Cut the spinach, *mitsuba*, or watercress into 2-inch lengths. If lily root is available, separate it into segments and boil in a little salted water for four to five minutes. Arrange the scallops, mushrooms and lily root segments on top of the bean curd.

Heat the broth and add it to the slightly beaten eggs, mixing well. Strain the custard and pour it carefully into the casseroles. Put the casseroles in a baking tin and pour boiling water in the tin until it comes halfway up their sides. Bake in a moderate oven for fifteen minutes. Remove and add the greens, pushing them gently down into the custard. Return to the oven and continue to bake until set. Serve hot.

HANJUKU-TAMAGO (Soft Boiled Eggs)

1 egg   Salt
½ teaspoon black sesame seeds

Submerge the egg in warm water for thirty minutes before cooking. Bring a saucepan of water to the boil and carefully drop in the egg and simmer for five minutes. Remove from the fire, leave in the hot water for thirty seconds and drain, then cool under cold water. Peel away the shells carefully and cut a tiny slice off each end so that the egg halves will stand upright. Cut the eggs in half with a length of thread (a knife will cling too much to the yolk). Arrange on a plate and sprinkle with a little salt and a few black sesame seeds. Serve warm or cool.

SCRAMBLED EGGS

4 eggs   Monosodium glutamate
2 teaspoons light soy sauce   2 tablespoons dried bonito
1 teaspoon sugar   shavings, *hanagatsuo* (optional)
Salt   1 tablespoon oil

Beat the eggs well and add all the other ingredients. Heat the oil in a frying pan and pour in the eggs. Cook over a medium flame, stirring constantly, until set. Remove to a serving plate and serve immediately.

DASHI-MAKI TAMAGO (*Rolled Omelet*)

6 eggs
½ cup *dashi* or other broth
1 tablespoon soy sauce

1 teaspoon sugar
Oil

Break the eggs into a bowl and beat well. Add the *dashi*, soy sauce, salt and sugar and beat until well mixed. Heat an omelet pan or rectangular frying pan (Japanese omelets are invariably fried in rectangular pans which makes the entire operation much easier to manage as well as resulting in a neater finished product). Lightly oil the frying pan which should be only moderately hot. Add one-third of the egg mixture and tilt the pan so that it covers the bottom evenly. When the egg mixture has become almost completely set (the top will still be slightly liquid) roll the omelet away from you into a neat cylinder, using either chopsticks or a spatula. Leave the rolled omelet in the pan and lightly oil the part of the frying pan which is now empty. Now slide the rolled omelet to the other side of the pan and oil the surface where it has been resting. Pour in half the remaining egg mixture, slightly raising the previously cooked omelet so that the raw egg can flow beneath it. When the egg mixture has become set repeat the operation above: roll the omelet, including the omelet already cooked, away from you into a single neat cylinder. Oil the pan and repeat the operation once more, cooking the remaining egg mixture. When the final egg is rolled up into the omelet you will have a thick cylinder about 2 inches in diameter. Remove the omelet to a bamboo mat (*sudare*) and roll the mat around the omelet, tying it with a little string. Let it stand for ten to fifteen minutes so that the circular shape of the omelet will be retained. Remove the bamboo mat and cut the omelet into slices about 1 inch thick. Serve at room temperature.

UMAKI (*Rolled Omelet Filled with Eel*)

2 eggs
2 tablespoons *dashi* or other broth
1 teaspoon soy sauce
Salt

Monosodium glutamate
1 piece *kabayaki* eel
Oil

Beat the eggs, add all the seasonings and mix well. Prepare the eel according to the recipe on page 100. Cut it into small pieces, roughly ½-inch cubes. Lightly oil the bottom of an omelet pan and heat. Add the eggs and cook over a moderate flame until set. Put the eel in a straight line across the omelet and roll it away from you. Turn out onto a plate and serve immediately, or turn out onto a *sudare* bamboo mat and roll firmly. Allow the omelet to stand for ten minutes, remove the mat and cut into slices about 1 inch thick. Serve at room temperature.

TORIMAKI (*Rolled Omelet Filled with Chicken*)

4 oz chopped cooked chicken
1 teaspoon finely chopped ginger root
2 teaspoons sugar
1 tablespoon soy sauce
1 tablespoon *mirin*

2 teaspoons cornflour
2 eggs
2 tablespoons *dashi* or other broth
1 teaspoon soy sauce
Salt
Monosodium glutamate

In this recipe a chicken filling is substituted for the eel filling in the recipe above. Mix together in small saucepan the chicken, ginger, sugar, soy sauce and *mirin*, and heat. Dissolve the cornflour in a little cold water and add to the saucepan, cooking until the mixture is thick and clear. Cool slightly and proceed as in the above recipe.

SPINACH EGG ROLLS

2 eggs
½ teaspoon salt
1 tablespoon oil

¼ lb raw spinach
2 tablespoons soy sauce

Wash the spinach and boil in salted water for three to four minutes, taking care not to overcook. Remove, drain and when cool enough to handle squeeze with the hands to remove any remaining water.

Beat the eggs and season with salt. Heat a little oil in an omelet pan or, preferably, a rectangular frying pan. When moderately hot pour in half the egg mixture, tilting the pan so that it covers the bottom evenly. Cook the omelet over low heat until set. Remove carefully and reserve. Cook the remaining egg mixture in the same way. Divide the spinach into half and arrange it in a line down the centre of each omelet. Roll the omelet over the spinach into a firm, neat cylinder. The cylinders are then cut into halves diagonally across the centre. Serve standing up with a little soy sauce poured over the top of the spinach. These spinach rolls are used as a garnish for fish or chicken.

IRITSUKEDŌFU (*Eggs and Bean Curd*)

1 square bean curd, *tōfu* (about 1 lb)
1 cup dried bonito shavings, *hanagatsuo*

5 tablespoons light soy sauce
3 tablespoons *mirin*
3 eggs
¼ teaspoon monosodium glutamate

Cut the bean curd into 1-inch cubes. Put the soy sauce, *mirin* and *hanagatsuo* into a saucepan with a fairly wide bottom and bring to the boil. Add the bean curd, cover and simmer for five minutes, until the bean curd is heated through. Beat the eggs and the monosodium glutamate together and pour over the bean curd. Cover with a lid and cook over a low fire until the eggs are set. Remove and serve immediately.

PICKLES

To us, that mysterious entity, 'real Japan', is not to be found in the tea ceremony, flower arrangements, or other traditional arts, or even in the Noh play or the Kabuki, the *haiku*, or the *geisha*. It is, rather, in quiet thatched farmhouses, under whose eaves vegetables and fruit hang in the long golden days of autumn, drying to muted but softly glowing colours before being preserved in the old ways. It is in the Shinto shrines, where stacked in colourful rows are the *sake* and pickle barrels with the manufacturers' names in bold black Chinese characters. Formerly these containers held the genuine article: now they are symbolic of cash donations, but the barrels are real enough. And it is above all in the covered markets where one smell pervades the atmosphere and dominates all others – the smell of Japanese pickles.

Every town in Japan produces some sort of *meibutsu* or noted product, and the foreigner visiting out-of-the-way places can derive a good deal of innocent amusement from inquiring politely of any inhabitant about the local *meibutsu*. One may confidently predict that not more than three or four places down the list, if not at the head, will be found 'pickles'. Of European countries only England can even begin to match the splendour or the variety of Japanese pickles. Every conceivable vegetable is steeped in brine, packed in redolent barrels in layers covered with rice bran and lovingly stored until matured. Then, penetratingly odoriferous, the pickles are bought in the market, sliced or chopped, and savoured as a relish, providing a sharp contrast to the bland and – dare it be said – rather boring taste of plain boiled rice.

In many low budget and country households, rice and pickles comprise the mid-day meal and a very bracing meal it can be, if the *tsukemono* are good. This 'main course' becomes the coda of a more expensive meal in Japan and sets a firm full stop to the seemingly endless procession of courses at a banquet. So important are pickles to the Japanese diet that we have provided a special section about them and stress the necessity of their appearance at virtually any meal that claims to be Japanese. Pickles are usually served in small individual dishes, neatly sliced or chopped. Two or three types are often combined in a single serving. A little soy sauce may be sprinkled over the top as desired.

CABBAGE RELISH

2 lb cabbage	¼ cup sugar
4 tablespoons white sesame seeds	2 teaspoons salt
1 cup vinegar	

Cut the cabbage into thin strips and put into a bowl. Toast the sesame seeds in a dry frying pan, stirring constantly, until they begin to jump. Mix together the vinegar, sugar, and salt and bring to a boil. Add the sesame seeds and cool. Pour the vinegar mixture over the cabbage and mix well. Put a plate or wooden lid on top of the cabbage and press it down with a 2 lb weight. Let stand for one to two hours before serving. In Japanese pickle-making a flat wooden lid, just smaller in diameter than the container, is always used. This allows uniform and firm pressure to be exerted, yet still enables moisture to escape around the sides.

KYŪRI MATSUMAE (Cucumbers Pickled in Soy Sauce)

2 lb cucumbers	3 dried red peppers
5 inches of *kombu* seaweed	½ cup soy sauce
(optional)	½ teaspoon monosodium glutamate

Thoroughly wash the cucumbers, slice off the ends but do not peel.

Split them in half lengthwise and remove the seeds. Cut in 1-inch lengths. Wash the *kombu* and slice into narrow strips. Slice the red peppers into narrow rings, about ⅛ inch wide. Put the cucumbers, seaweed and red peppers into a bowl, sprinkle the soy sauce and monosodium glutamate over them and toss lightly until well covered. Place on top of the cucumbers a plate or wooden lid and press it down with a 2 lb weight. Leave twelve to twenty-four hours before serving. Do not wash before serving.

CAULIFLOWER AND GREEN PEPPER RELISH

2 lb cauliflower	¼ cup sugar
2 green peppers	1½ teaspoons salt
1 cup vinegar	

Separate the cauliflower into flowerlets and soak in cold salted water for thirty minutes. Slice the green peppers into thin strips. Bring a saucepan of water to the boil and dip the cauliflower and green peppers into the boiling water, remove after two or three seconds and drain well. Put vegetables into a glass or earthenware bowl and sprinkle with salt. Mix together the vinegar, sugar, salt and monosodium glutamate and bring to the boil. Allow it to cool slightly. Pour over the cauliflower and green peppers and toss lightly. Put a plate or lid on top of the vegetables, press down with a 2 lb weight and allow to stand for five to six hours. Do not wash before serving.

CHINESE CABBAGE RELISH

½ head of Chinese cabbage (about 1½ lb)	½ lemon
1 red pepper	¼ cup soy sauce
1 spring onion	½ cup vinegar
	½ teaspoon monosodium glutamate

Separate the leaves of the cabbage and cut into strips about 1 inch wide and 2 inches long. Put in a colander, pour boiling water over the top and drain thoroughly. Mince the spring onion, including green top. Cut the red pepper into thin rings. Slice the lemon into thin rounds, then into strips. Put the cabbage, spring onion, red pepper, and lemon into a bowl and pour over them the soy sauce and vinegar and sprinkle on the monosodium glutamate. Toss the vegetables lightly until well covered with the dressing. Place a plate or wooden lid on top of the cabbage and press down with a 1½ lb weight for one to two hours before serving.

EGGPLANT RELISH

1 lb eggplant	1½ tablespoons *mirin*
Salt	3 tablespoons soy sauce
1 tablespoon mustard	¼ teaspoon monosodium glutamate

Slice the eggplant and sprinkle liberally with salt. Let stand for thirty minutes. Drain away the excess water and dry with a clean cloth. Mix the mustard to a smooth paste with a little water and add the *mirin* and the soy sauce. Put the eggplant in a bowl, pour the mustard dressing over the top and toss lightly. Put a wooden lid or a plate on top of the eggplants and press down with a 1 lb weight. Leave for one to two hours. To serve, chop in small pieces and arrange in individual dishes.

RAKKYO-ZUKE (*Pickled Onions*)

5 lb pearl onions	½ lb rock sugar
3–4 oz salt	6–7 red peppers
1 quart vinegar	

Carefully skin the onions, roll them in the salt and put them into a clean jar with a lid. Allow to stand for three days, by which time a great deal of moisture will have accumulated in the jar. Drain the onions and return to the jar. Bring the vinegar and rock sugar to the boil, remove from the fire and pour over the onions. The rock sugar will not be completely dissolved but that does not matter. The onions should be completely covered by the vinegar mixture. Add the red peppers. Cover the jar with a paper lid, tying it tightly around the neck of the jar. Allow the onions to stand for about three months before eating

BENI-SHŌGA (*Pickled Ginger*)

5 lb fresh ginger roots   1 quart vinegar
3 oz salt   ½ lb rock sugar

This pickle is prepared in the same way as the onions above. Wash the
ginger roots, scrubbing the surface well and peeling any skin which is
especially discoloured. Then proceed as above. A little plum juice is
often added to the vinegar in order to dye the ginger pink.

TAKUAN (*Pickled Daikon Radish*)

The pungent, almost rancid smell of *takuan* is unmistakable and hovers
over monastery kitchens as invariably as the scent of incense fills the
temples themselves. Its associations with Buddhism still run deep. The
priest Takuan introduced it into the Japanese diet in the seventeenth
century and since that time it has become the most common of all
pickles, so much a part of everyday life, indeed, that the term 'rice and
takuan' have become synonymous with frugality.

3–4 Japanese radish, *daikon*   1 lb salt
3 quarts water   4 lb rice bran, *nuka*

Wash the *daikon* and hang them in a cool, dry, shaded place for two to
three weeks. Mix the *nuka* with the water. Put a layer of *nuka* in the
bottom of a pickling barrel, sprinkle over it a layer of salt and arrange on
top a whole *daikon*. Cover with *nuka*, add another layer of salt, *daikon*
and *nuka* and continue in this fashion until all the radishes are arranged
in the barrel. Finish with a layer of *nuka*. Press down a wooden lid on
top of the ingredients in the barrel and put on top of the lid a weight of
the same weight as the *daikon*. Allow to pickle for at least one month
before eating.

HAKUSAI NO SHIOZUKE (*Pickled Chinese Cabbage*)

1 head of Chinese cabbage   Wooden pickling barrel
Salt

Wash the cabbage thoroughly under cold running water. Slice through the bottom of the cabbage, separating the head into six or eight lengths. Sprinkle a good handful of salt on the bottom of the barrel. Arrange the cabbage on top of the salt with the cut surface facing upwards. Alternate stem and leaves so that they can be packed more firmly into the barrel. Sprinkle with another good handful of salt, and then add another layer of cabbage, alternating layers of salt and cabbage until the cabbage is all used. Put on top of the cabbage a wooden lid, slightly smaller than the barrel so that it can press directly onto the cabbage and salt. Press the lid down with a stone weighing approximately the same amount as the cabbage. Let the cabbage stand. In about twenty-four hours water will begin to appear around the lid. Let the cabbage stand for two to three days longer and it is then ready to eat.

To serve, remove from the salt and wash under running cold water. Squeeze out the water with your hands. Chop the cabbage into small pieces and serve in a small bowl accompanied by a bowl of plain hot rice. If desired, a little soy sauce and/or monosodium glutamate may be sprinkled over the top.

KARASHINA NO SHIOZUKE (Pickled Mustard Leaves)

2 lb mustard greens   Salt
Wooden pickling barrel

Wash the mustard greens thoroughly. Bring a large saucepan of water to the boil and dip the greens into it, removing immediately and rinsing under cold water. Drain thoroughly, then proceed as in the recipe above. The mustard greens will take about the same time to pickle as Chinese cabbage.

NUKA NO TSUKEMONO (Vegetable Cured in Rice Bran)

4 lb rice bran, *nuka*   ½ lb salt
6 cups water   4 slices bread
Vegetable to be pickled

Put the rice bran in a dry frying pan and heat, stirring constantly, until it is dry, warm and slightly toasted. Boil together the water and salt and cool. Pour half the rice bran into a mixing bowl and pour in the salt water. Mix thoroughly and add the remaining rice bran, again mixing well. Tear the bread into small pieces, add to the *nuka* mixture and mix well. The purpose of this is to add a small amount of yeast to the mixture, a step which is unnecessary in professional pickle-making where the *nuka* used is sometimes as much as ten years old, a guarantee that it has developed its own yeasty properties. Put the rice bran mixture into a glass or earthenware container.

Wash thoroughly the vegetables to be pickled. Almost any vegetable may be used including cabbage, cucumber, eggplant, watermelon rind, radish, turnip, green pepper and Chinese cabbage. Cut the vegetables into large pieces, about 3 inches by 1½ inches in diameter. Rub salt into their surface. This not only adds flavour but preserves the vegetable's natural colour. Bury the vegetables in the rice bran mixture and let them cure for twelve to twenty-four hours. Cover the container. Remove the vegetables, rinse off the *nuka* under running water and drain thoroughly, pressing to remove excess water. Chop or slice into thin pieces and serve with a sprinkling of soy sauce and monosodium glutamate.

The *nuka* mixture may be kept indefinitely if cared for properly. Once or twice a day turn it with the hands or with a spoon in order to add air, and then smooth down the top.

GREEN PEPPERS PICKLED IN BEAN PASTE

10–12 green peppers	⅓ cup *mirin*
1 teaspoon salt	2 tablespoons *sake*
1 lb white bean paste, *shiro-miso*	½ teaspoon monosodium glutamate

Bring a saucepan of salted water to the boil and add the green peppers, boiling for one minute. Remove and drain. Remove seeds and tops and cut lengthwise into 1-inch widths. Mix together the bean paste, *mirin*, *sake* and monosodium glutamate. Spread one-half the bean paste mixture on the bottom of a wooden container and put a layer of peppers on top. Cover with the remaining bean paste. Leave in a cool, dark place, or in the refrigerator, for one week. To serve, rinse off the bean paste, cut into small pieces and serve with a little soy sauce.

BEVERAGES

Tea

The Japanese have been drinking tea since the ninth century, and are as devoted to it as the English. The beverage pervades every aspect of life, from the sacred to the profane. Its preparation and drinking takes on a quasi-religious character in temples and in the formal tea ceremony, while the tea-houses in which geisha entertain their patrons still provide tea, as well as more authoritative beverages.

In day-to-day life, a filled teapot stands on every dining-table during every meal, and a cup of tea is the invariable accompaniment to any conversation, business or social. Though Japanese do drink imported 'western-style' or 'black' tea with lemon or milk, and the name of Lipton is famous throughout the land, Japanese tea is still more popular. It is always green, i.e. the leaves are dried but not fermented. It somewhat resembles China tea and is similarly drunk plain, without milk or sugar.

There are four main types of Japanese teas: *gyokuro, sencha, bancha,* and *matcha. Gyokuro* tea is reckoned to be the aristocrat of them all and consists of the first picking of the youngest and most tender leaves. It is strong and is drunk with cakes or served to special guests. Use about four heaping tablespoons of the tea to two cups water, which should have been boiled and cooled to a temperature of 160° F before pouring it over the leaves. Allow to brew for three to five minutes and serve.

Sencha is also commonly served with cakes or to guests and is of a slightly inferior quality, but not quite so bitter as *gyokuro*. Use four heaping tablespoons of tea to three cups water. The water should be boiled and cooled to a temperature of 175° F before pouring it over the leaves.

Bancha, which is simply the inferior leaves and stems left after picking *sencha*, is brewed in the same way as *sencha*, using slightly less tea and pouring boiling water straight onto the leaves. It is the most commonly drunk beverage in Japan and is always served with rice, the varieties above being too concentrated in flavour to drink in any quantity. All three of these teas can be steeped two or three times before discarding the leaves.

Matcha, or *hikicha* as it is sometimes called, is the powdered green tea used in the tea ceremony. Put three heaping teaspoons of the powder into a tea bowl, pour in hot water and whip (in the tea ceremony a bamboo whisk resembling a shaving brush is used for this operation) until smooth.

Sake

Conventional grape wines have been made in Japan for a very long time. The best reds and whites are palatable enough, but of no distinction, while Japanese 'champagne' has been described not unjustly as being ideal for launching ships. Although large quantities of western-style alcoholic drinks are both produced in Japan and imported, there can be no doubt that *sake* remains the pre-eminent national drink.

It is, moreover, the sacramental wine of Shinto, the old animistic system of customs and observances which preceded Buddhism and has survived alongside it. Nearly all weddings are conducted according to Shinto rites, and the marriage contract is sealed when bride and groom exchange and drink from *sake* cups in the 'thrice-three' ceremony.

Cold *sake* which has been spiced is always drunk ceremoniously on New Year's Day, which is without question the most important day of the year; and there are many other occasions when its use is prescribed by hallowed tradition.

Sake is produced in various grades, of which the cheapest, coarsest and lowest in alcoholic strength is 'second class'. 'First class' is better in all respects, but 'special grade' is much the best for pleasurable drinking. Some brewers produce a 'super-special grade' *sake*, which even on occasion has a few flakes of gold leaf floating in it. It is beautifully packaged and makes an elegant present, but is not noticeably better to drink than 'special'.

As with Scotch, much depends on the water which is used to make *sake*. That of the Nada area near Kobe is particularly good, and Nada *sake* is renowned all over Japan. It is clean and vigorous to the palate, and is thought to be masculine in character. An equally famous 'feminine' partner is the *sake* made in Fushimi, just south of Kyoto, and much favoured in that city not only for reasons of local patriotism but because its shy, gentle taste seems to match very well the classical charms of the geisha who pour it so elegantly for their patrons. Excellent *sake* is also made in Hiroshima, and almost every district of Japan produces a locally popular brand.

The alcoholic content of even the best *sake* is not much higher than that of ordinary grape wine. Since it is customarily served at about blood heat, a good deal even of the original alcohol has evaporated by the time it is drunk. Nevertheless, *sake* has an agreeably encouraging effect and a little goes a remarkably long way with most Japanese. Westerners, with their greater intake of fat, seem to find it much more difficult to get tight on *sake*.

The *sake* exported to the West often contains a preservative to maintain its palatability beyond the year in which it is made, but care should always be taken not to buy old stock. The method of serving *sake* has already been described, but since it is so simple we repeat it here. If you possess authentic *sake* flasks and cups, use them of course. If not, fill a small narrow jug with about ½ pint of *sake*, and stand it in hot water until the *sake* is roughly at blood heat. Drink it from small liqueur glasses replenished frequently while the next jug is warming. *Kampai!*

TAMAGO-ZAKE (*Sake Eggnog*)

This is an excellent bed-time posset to ward off the winter cold or the common cold. Serves one.

1 egg	½ pint *sake*
1 tablespoon honey	

Beat the egg and honey well in a sturdy beaker which has been well warmed. In the meantime pour the *sake* straight into a small saucepan and bring it almost to boiling point. Pour on to the egg and honey in a thin stream, stirring vigorously to avoid curdling. Drink at once.

AMAZAKE (Sweet Sake)

Amazake is a very popular cold-weather drink made from the rice lees left over from *sake* brewing. Its texture is very like that of thin porridge. Its alcoholic content is practically nil, but it has a yeasty reminiscence of *sake* which is most pleasant.

1 package *kōji*, rice lees (about 3 loosely packed cups)	Sugar Salt
1 cup *mochigome* or ordinary rice	Grated ginger root
3 cups water	

Put the rice and water in a saucepan, bring to the boil, cover and cook slowly until the rice is very tender and its consistency is about the same as porridge. Cool to lukewarm. Then add the *kōji*, mix thoroughly and cover. Put in a warm place; ideally, it should ferment in a place where the temperature is about the same as that required for yeast dough to rise, about 80° to 85° F. If it is too warm the mixture will sour. Let the mixture stand for three to four days, mixing once or twice each day. When it smells yeasty and both the rice and *kōji* are extremely soft it is ready to drink.

To serve add 2 cups water to 1 cup *amazake* mixture and heat. When very hot add sugar to taste and a pinch of salt. Pour into a glass or mug and add $\frac{1}{2}$ to 1 teaspoon grated ginger. Mix and serve immediately.

UMESHU (Plum Wine)

$2\frac{1}{2}$ lb green plums	2 quarts *shōchū*, a rough distilled spirit of about 40 per cent alcohol, or vodka
$3\frac{1}{2}$ lb rock sugar	

Wash the plums carefully and let them soak in cold water for one hour. Dry thoroughly with a clean cloth and prick the skin of each plum several times with a fork. Take a jar large enough to hold all the plums and wash and dry it thoroughly. Put a layer of plums on the bottom of the jar and sprinkle over them a good handful of the sugar. Add another layer of plums and sugar, repeating until the jar is full. Pour the *shōchū* over the top. Cover and seal very tightly. Put in a cool dark place and let the wine mature for several months. It can be drunk when the sugar has dissolved, but is best drunk at about one year.

Sweet and Sour Prawns
Beef Sukiyaki
Boiled Rice
Pickles
Fresh Fruit

Clear Soup with Chicken and
    Mushrooms
Fish Teriyaki
Vegetables Boiled with Chicken
Lotus Root Salad
Boiled Rice
Pickles

Clear Soup with Prawn and
    Watercress
Salmon Baked in Foil
Combination Salad with Golden
    Dressing
Rice and Ginger

Miso Soup with Pork and
    Burdock Root
Tempura
Radish and Carrot Salad
Rice
Pickles

Clear Soup with Bamboo Shoots
    and Seaweed
Sake Chicken
Garnished Rice
Sautéed Green Peppers
Cucumber and Seaweed Salad
Fresh Fruit

Chawan Mushi
Nigiri-zushi
Spinach and Apple Salad

Sashimi
Egg Drop Soup
Fish Baked on Pine Needles
Spinach with Sesame Seeds
Autumn Salad

Clear Soup with Clams and
    Mushrooms
Fish Grilled with Salt
Bamboo Shoots and Chicken
    Dumplings
Rice and Mushrooms
White Salad

Fish Cured in Bean Paste
Odamaki Mushi
Chrysanthemum Turnips
Omelet and Spinach Rolls

Clear Soup with Quail Egg and
    Vegetables
Chicken Teriyaki
Sautéed Mushrooms and
    Cucumbers
Bamboo Shoot Salad
Rice
Pickles

Kuzuhiki Soup
Mackerel Simmered in Soy Sauce
Raw Fish and Cucumber Salad
Boiled Bamboo Shoots
Rice
Pickles

Hiyashi Sōmen (Chilled Noodles)
Harusame Tempura
Celery, Cucumber and Scallop
    Salad with Golden Dressing

MAKUNOUCHI BENTO (BOXED LUNCH)

Rice Onigiri
Thick Rolled Omelet
Prawns Onigara
Fish Cured in Bean Paste

Spinach with Peanuts
Braised Lotus Root
Chicken Croquettes

KAISEKI (BANQUET)

1st course – Clear Soup   Clear Soup with Herrings
2nd course – Raw Fish   Sashimi
3rd course – Appetizer   Scallop and Spring Onion Salad
4th course – Grilled Fish   Trout Grilled in Salt
5th course – Boiled Food   Bamboo Shoots and Chicken Dumplings
6th course – Vinegared Food   Cucumber and Crab Salad
7th course – Steamed Food   Steamed Egg Custard with Eel
              Boiled Rice
              Pickles
              Miso Soup

aburage	fried bean curd
aemono	salad
agemono	food fried in deep oil
Aji-no-moto	monosodium glutamate
aka-miso	red bean paste
anago	sea eel; conger eel
awabi	abalone
ayu	small river trout
beni-shōga	red, pickled ginger
castera	sponge cake
chirimen-zako	small cooked fish which are eaten whole
chūka-nabe	Chinese concave frying pan
daikon	white radish
dango	dumpling, meat ball, or croquette
dashi	basic Japanese soup stock
donabe	earthenware casserole
ebi	prawn
ginnan	gingko nut
ginshi-yaki	the technique of cooking in aluminium foil
gobō	burdock root
goma	sesame seed
goma-abura	sesame seed oil
hakusai	Chinese cabbage
hamaguri	clams
hanagatsuo	dried bonito shavings
harusame	noodles made from soybean flour
hashi	chopsticks
hōrensō	spinach
ika	cuttlefish, squid
jaga-imo	potato
kabocha	pumpkin, squash

kaibashira	scallops
kaki	oysters
kamaboko	fish sausage
kampyō	dried gourd shavings
kara-age	literally 'dry-frying'; the method of dusting food in cornflour and frying in deep oil
karashi	mustard
katsuobushi	dried bonito fillet
kimisu	salad dressing made from egg yolks and vinegar
kinome	leaf of the prickly ash, used as a garnish and for seasoning
kisu	smelts
kōji	rice lees
kombu	kelp seaweed
konnyaku	devil's tongue
kōyadōfu	dried bean curd
kuri	chestnuts
kushi-age	the technique of impaling food on skewers and frying in deep oil
maguro	tuna
matcha	powdered green tea, used in the tea ceremony
matsutake	*armillaria edocles* mushroom
menrui	generic term for noodles
mirin	sweetened rice wine used in cooking
miso	bean paste
misozuke	vegetables pickled in bean paste
mitsuba	trefoil, a pungent herb used as a garnish and in soups
moyashi	bean sprouts
mushimono	steamed food
nabemono	literally 'pot-thing'; refers to any meal cooked in one dish
na-no-hana	blossoms of the rape plant, used as a garnish and sometimes pickled
naganegi	spring onions (or shallots)
namazake	fresh salmon
nasu	eggplant
negi	onion

niboshi	small dried fish resembling sardines
nimono	boiled food
ninjin	carrot
nira	chives
ninniku	garlic
nitsuke	the technique of simmering fish or vegetables in soy sauce and sugar
nori	purple laver seaweed
nuka	rice bran
ocha	green tea
omochi	rice cake
oshiwaku	wooden box for pressing *sushi*
piman	green pepper
renkon	lotus root
saba	mackerel
sakazuki	*sake* cup
sake	rice wine
sansho	Japanese spice, made from the leaf of the prickly ash
sato-imo	taro
satsuma-imo	sweet potato
sawara	delicious fish of the mackerel family
sembei	rice wafers, flavoured with soy sauce or other seasonings and served with drinks
seri	a kind of parsley grown in water, *oenanthe stolonthe*
shichimi-tōgarashi	seven-flavour seasoning
shiitake	dried mushroom
shiozuke	vegetables pickled in salt
shirataki	a translucent noodle made from the roots of the devil's tongue plant
shiro-miso	white bean paste
shirumono	soup
shiso	beefsteak plant, the leaves of which are used as a pickle and a garnish
shōga	ginger
shōjin-ryōri	Buddhist vegetarian cooking
shōyu	soy sauce
shungiku	edible chrysanthemum leaves

soba	noodles made from buckwheat flour
sōmen	a thin noodle made from wheat flour
su	vinegar
sudare	bamboo mat used for rolling foods
suimono	clear soup
sunomono	literally 'vinegared things'; salads
suribachi	earthenware mortar with serrated interior surface
suzuke	vegetables pickled in vinegar
tai	red sea bream
takenoko	bamboo shoots
tara	cod
teriyaki	the technique of grilling foods while basting with a sauce of soy sauce and *mirin*
tōfu	bean curd
tōgan	Chinese winter melon
tōgarashi	hot red pepper
toso	*sake* spiced with herbs and drunk cold at New Year's
tsukemono	pickles
tsukeyaki	the technique of marinating foods in soy sauce and other seasonings, then briefly sautéeing or grilling
udon	noodle made of wheat flour
unagi	eel
uni	sea urchin or sea chestnut; also used to refer to the paste made from this shellfish
ushiojiru	clear soup made from fish or shellfish
wakame	lobe-leaf seaweed
warabi	bracken, edible fern sprout used in soups and salads
waribashi	wooden chopsticks
wasabi	horseradish
yakidōfu	grilled soy bean curd
yakimono	grilled foods
yudōfu	boiled soy bean curd
yurine	lily bulb
yuzu	citron
zaru	bamboo colander

INDEX